ART of the PIE

KATE McDERMOTT

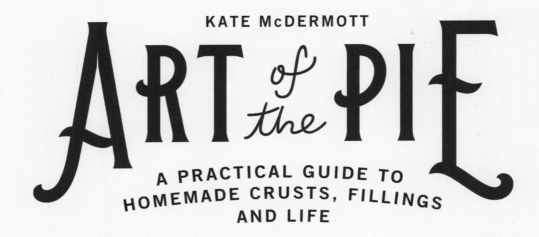

ART of the PIE

A PRACTICAL GUIDE TO HOMEMADE CRUSTS, FILLINGS AND LIFE

Photographs by
ANDREW SCRIVANI

THE COUNTRYMAN PRESS
· · · · ·
A division of W. W. Norton & Company
Independent Publishers Since 1923

For information about permission to reproduce selections from this book, write to
Permissions, The Countryman Press, 500 Fifth Avenue, New York, NY 10110

For information about special discounts for bulk purchases, please contact
W. W. Norton Special Sales at specialsales@wwnorton.com or 800-233-4830

Book design by Nick Caruso Design
Manufacturing through Asia Pacific Offset

Library of Congress Cataloging-in-Publication Data

Names: McDermott, Kate, 1953- author. | Scrivani, Andrew, photographer.
Title: Art of the pie : a practical guide to homemade crusts, fillings, and
    life / Kate McDermott ; photographs by Andrew Scrivani.
Description: New York, NY : Countryman Press, a division of W. W. Norton &
    Company, Independent Publishers Since 1923, [2016] | Includes
    bibliographical references and index.
Identifiers: LCCN 2016017593 | ISBN 9781581573275 (hardcover)
Subjects: LCSH: Pies. | LCGFT: Cookbooks.
Classification: LCC TX773 .M343 2016 | DDC 641.86/52—dc23 LC record available at
    https://lccn.loc.gov/2016017593

The Countryman Press
www.countrymanpress.com

A division of W. W. Norton & Company, Inc.
500 Fifth Avenue, New York, NY 10110
www.wwnorton.com

10 9 8 7 6 5 4

For Duncan, the apple of my eye.

CONTENTS

INTRODUCTION

I like being known as a pie maker; there is a certain humble hominess to it. It's one of life's pursuits that I feel good about mastering and likely will always continue to practice. It's something I do with my hands and heart. It harms none and maybe brings a little joy and happiness to the world, too. But what I like even more than making pie is teaching the art of pie making. In some ways, I feel that pie has chosen me to pass on this time-honored craft to as many as I can.

Although I have never sold a pie in my life, I have taught thousands across the country how simple and fun pie making can be. If one is available, I will give a slice—or even an entire pie—to anyone who shows up at my door, and as a practitioner of this craft on a near-daily basis, chances are that those who make the pilgrimage to my Pie Cottage home will leave satisfied. Giving is a big part of my practice.

Pie has been a taskmaster, a teacher, and a healer for me. I've learned a lot from this vocation, and in some ways I feel that its life lessons have saved me from some very challenging times. Each time I make a pie, I feel an unbroken line of pie makers who have come before me, pouring their tears, laughter, and wisdom into me and right out through my hands. With each stroke of the rolling pin, I hear them say, "Pass on this craft. Pass on what we share with you." I believe anyone can make pie, and over the years I have taught thousands to do so. Although some beg to differ on the difficulty factor, this is pie making, not rocket science. As the saying goes, "It's Easy as Pie." Sometimes it's just a matter of belief and trust. Here's how it all began for me . . .

My grandmother was the pie maker in our family. She didn't want to be labeled anything remotely indicating her status as an elder, so she settled on Geeg, pronounced "Jeedge." Born in 1896, Geeg was the youngest of six daughters raised on an Iowa farm. She eloped at age eighteen, and had two children soon after. As a mother, she baked for her family; as a grandmother, she baked for all our family gatherings: apple for every day, pumpkin for Thanksgiving, and lemon meringue with just the right balance of tart and sweet to chase the blues away.

Geeg lived with us, so I knew her no-nonsense ways pretty darn well. She was deliberate and to the point. She could always find a way to do what was needed. Self taught, she had a knack and way with dough and fillings. I wish she had written down her recipes, but she never did because she didn't need to. Deep inside she simply knew how it was done. I was honored to be present for the last pie she ever made.

On that day, we were gathered in the kitchen—my mother, my brother, and me. Geeg was flustered and it became clear to us that something out of the ordinary had happened. Nothing seemed to make sense to her. She didn't know where she was or what to do. We didn't know it then, but she had suffered a stroke. While my brother and mom debated about calling for medical care, out of the blue I asked, "Geeg, can you make a pie?" She stopped in her tracks, looked directly at me with light blue eyes that could see deep into you, and said, "Well, yes!" She seemed calmed by the thought; pie was something she knew as

well as the back of her broad and wrinkled hand.

I placed ice water, flour, salt, her big blue can of Crisco, and my mom's yellow Pyrex mixing bowl on the pull-out breadboard, and she turned to her work: first the flour and the salt, then the shortening—spoonful after spoonful went into the bowl. There must have been more fat than flour, but she always said that using so much of it was what gave her a very flaky crust. She added ice water from a glass, a tablespoon at a time, just enough to hold it all together.

Without waiting to chill the dough in the icebox, as both she and my mom called the refrigerator, she moved right on to rolling. Maybe she knew that time was of the essence, and that this would be the last pie she would ever make. Geeg scattered a handful of flour onto the breadboard scarred with decades of hatch-marks from cutting sandwiches in halves and quarters for our school lunch pails. She tossed a bit more onto the top of the dough and began to roll. Back and forth, out and back—there was a rhythm to it. Then, stopping and turning her gaze to me, I saw that her eyes were moist and tears had started to run down her soft cheeks. Without a word, she gave her red handled rolling pin to me to finish the job. Geeg had passed her pie mantle to me.

Say the word "pie" and it brings to mind home, the fragrance of an apple harvest, the crunch of dry leaves on a crisp autumn day, summer picnics spread out on a red plaid tablecloth, memories of family gatherings around the table, and late-night trips to the kitchen for just one more piece. Family, friends, tradition, flavor—how can something as humble as pie have the power to hold all this inside a simple pastry shell? And yet, it holds all of this and more. Pie is a comfort and balm to many a weary soul. I can't imagine any other food that symbolizes as much happiness and love. Perhaps it exists as part of our collective consciousness, because whether we are baking, sharing, or eating pie, we seem to tap into something that is much greater than the sum of its baked ingredients. We view pie as such an American icon that food writer John T. Edge has said, "If I were to create a coat of arms for our country, a pie would be its heraldic symbol."

Pie is generous and adaptable. It offers a never-ending stream of variations on the theme of pastry with filling, both savory and sweet. I make pies and give them away—to my family, to my friends, to my community.

Pie is a meditation that I have practiced countless times. Some of my first attempts were less than stellar, but I didn't give up because I felt something drawing me in. Standing at the baking counter ready to put my hands into a bowl filled with flour, salt, fat, and water has become a contemplative part of my day—and one that I look forward to.

Pie is the best teacher I've ever had.

I learn something new about dough, or rolling, or filling each time I'm at the baking counter. I regularly hear from my students, "I thought I was coming to learn to make pie, but I learned a lot about myself, too." I don't consider myself an expert, but instead a devoted practitioner of the craft. My lessons at the baking counter continue to this day, and what I've learned I feel compelled to share with others. The challenge of mastering a flaky crust didn't come overnight, but it was not as hard as I was first led to believe.

Pie is an ambassador of love. Pie doesn't care about perfection or precision. It doesn't care if it's savory or sweet, big or little, or whether it is finished with a full top or a lattice top. Although nice for the baker, pie couldn't care less if it merits a blue ribbon at the fair. What matters is that it continues to be made, shared, and taught so that there will be an unbroken line of future generations of pie makers practicing the craft. When you put all of that together, pie teaches us that—far more important than the right sugar, or ratio of fat to flour—love is the most important ingredient. Made with hands and hearts, pie is love, and love is best when shared. "When you can make a good pie, you will have a special gift to give others that money can't buy," wrote Marion Cunningham. So on that coat of arms I would add a banner bearing the words "All you need is love." And in the end, that really is what it's all about.

Kate's Rules of Pie Making and Life

I rely on a common-sense approach to my craft and to life. Try everything. If it works . . . great. If it doesn't work . . . that's great, too. Either way, I will have learned something, including the lesson of not retrying something that didn't work the first time around. In my pie life, that includes times like the day I left the whipping cream in the stand mixer while cooking up a filling on the stove. By the time I remembered the mixer, the white cream had turned into yellow butter. Or the day I overfilled my pie pan with a delicious fruit filling only to have much of the juice spill out onto the oven floor during the bake and set off smoke alarms just before company arrived. When I forget such a no-brainer, you may see me hitting my head on the baking counter. Although, when I can do a nifty save and swerve out of the direct path of pie failure so that no one ever knows the pie and I were courting disaster, I get a little pie-high. My "brilliant" ideas aren't always brilliant, but most everything is worth trying once, especially if you get some lovely homemade butter in the process.

With many years of practice at the baking counter, I have developed three simple rules that work for pie making and life. Because I feel they are important to remember, you'll see them pop up more than once throughout these pages.

Rule #1: Keep Everything Chilled, Especially Yourself

Chill your dough, the flour, the fats, your pastry cloth, the bowl you make your dough in, even the work bowl and blade of your food processor if you're not doing it by hand . . . what am I missing here? Only the most important chill of all. Yourself! Pie making, like life, can be approached in a number of different ways, and if you are uptight about your pie dough, fussing and fretting over every little tug and tear, you are probably expending energy you simply don't need to. Perfection is one of those things that can drive people crazy. My creative side gets plugged up when there is chaos around me, so, taking care of myself the best way I can, I find ways to navigate around it. This is my own first step to a sense of inner peace. This practice has given me enough flexibility in my life to change directions mid-stream when necessary, which has happened more than once in unexpected and sometimes unwelcome ways. When I remember not to take things so darn personally, I'm usually fine.

When things are in order and perking along nicely, I try to experience every minute fully because I know that life can change in an instant. When I was younger and the carpet was pulled out from under me, I thought life as I knew it was over, never to be the same. And you know what? I was right. It wasn't ever the same. I took big steps and leaps, sometimes willingly and sometimes not, onto new paths. I had to either embrace new

dreams or stay stuck in the muck of old ones that had become nightmares. I remember my mom telling me that I could be exasperatingly stubborn like my grandmother. I had to learn things for myself, so my lessons included getting stuck in relationships, jobs, or living situations that may have been right for me once, but served me no longer. When I was finally able to turn a corner and continue on my own path, new and exciting experiences opened up for me that I would have missed had I stayed. I've lived six decades now and I know life's inevitable low spots are not permanent. They are never permanent— unless I stubbornly let them be. There are lessons in these less graceful times, too, and knowing that I'm only here . . . or there . . . for a short time, I can make the most of whatever lesson is right in front of me. I accept the downs, as well as the ups, hopefully with enough grace and gratitude that I can later share with others what I have learned along the way. Laugh a little more. Smile a lot more. Be content in believing that wherever you are, and whatever you are doing, it is never worth getting so worked up over it that you lose your mind, your health, or your spirit. Pie is a simple reminder that some days you will be at the peak of your game, like when you bake up a beauty that could be on a magazine cover. On other days it's okay to give yourself a break and lighten up; maybe ask for help and even accept it when it comes—and come it most definitely will, usually in a way you least expect. When dough gets tough, it might be because of overthinking and overworking. Work dough and life lightly; just enough for it to come together, so you can roll along. And always remember to keep everything chilled, especially yourself.

Rule #2: Keep Your Boundaries

Kitchen counter edges, pie plate edges . . . life's edges.

Through the years, I have willingly cared for family, pets, and friends, as well as worked more than full-time to pay the bills. I have found great satisfaction and meaning in caring for others; it's just a basic part of who I am. One can reach a line where giving too much support, without caring for one's own self, helps no one at all. I may also be taking away someone else's opportunity to have important life lessons and experiences of their own. In the past, I counseled friends to honor their boundaries, sometimes forgetting or never truly learning that I needed to honor my own first.

You might wonder how this relates to pie. It's really pretty easy. If pie dough droops over the edge of the pie pan it may melt and burn on the sides—and although unseen, the rim of the crust may also burn underneath. In my own life, I thought my boundaries could expand forever. I didn't know where they were because I had pushed past them long ago. I simply ignored warning signs, not willing to see how deeply and invisibly burned I had become.

I know where my pie's edges are and give special attention to them when adding the finishing touches. After trimming the bottom and top dough to about a half inch beyond the rim of the pan, I give them a quick fold towards the center to make a little reservoir that will keep all the juices of the fruit filling safely inside the pan. I take my open palms and lightly pat all the way around the edges, so my dough gets the idea that it is round, like a pie. At the same time, I move the dough a quarter of an inch or so away from the edge of the pie. Next, I give a final crimp or flute, making sure I can still see that safe boundary of plate completely encircling my pie. I tidy up the edge by running a clean cloth around to wipe away any extra flour, fat, and sugar, and then pop my pie into the oven knowing that I have taken care of it as best I can.

Thinking about how I handle something as simple as finishing the edges of a pie helps me pay attention to the boundaries of my own life. It took a lot of work to rein myself back in and away from the precipice I was looking over at the end of a challenging marriage.

In finding and observing my boundaries, I now ask myself:

- Does this work for me?
- Do I feel happy and content around those who are in my life?
- Do I have enough energy to help another, or do I need to give more care to myself?

Because I need lots of help remembering that it's okay to have boundaries, I practice on pie. It's simple, humble, and forgiving. Learn where your own boundaries are. Give yourself some extra care and space . . . the rest will follow.

Rule #3: Vent

"If you don't have anything nice to say, don't say anything at all." These are words I was raised with; maybe you were, too. Sometimes this is good advice. In fact, much of the time it is a tenet that I hold right up there with the Golden Rule, the one that goes, "Do unto others as you would have them do unto you." I think that's a pretty important rule, too. But, there have been times when I was about to boil over and had no emotional outlet—or at least I thought I didn't. Well, my body found a way to express it: with illness. Had I realized that it is okay to vent, if done in an appropriate and constructive manner, I might have saved myself a lot of pain. You don't want the filling of your pie to erupt like Mount Vesuvius in places where the dough is weak or patched. So, cut a few vents on the top of the pie to let the steam out. If you need to vent more, cut some more vents, or make a lattice crust to let out even more steam. You and your pie will feel a whole lot better.

Tools of the Trade or Mise-en-Pie

The tools I use for pie making are simple and most of them can be found in any kitchen:

- a bowl
- a cup
- a knife
- a spoon
- a fork
- a glass
- a rolling pin
- a pie pan
- plastic wrap
- a favorite apron
- a tea towel
- and a smile . . . that's the most important part.

I set up my workspace much like setting a place at the table. In the center, I place a bowl that is large enough for me to comfortably get my hands into. On the left, I place a fork for mixing dough. On the right, there is a knife for cutting butter, trimming the edges, and making lattice strips and vents; a spoon for mixing the filling; a cup for measuring dry and wet ingredients; and a glass of ice water. I tuck my pie pan underneath my work bowl, and behind them I place my rolling pin. I put on my apron, place a towel over my left shoulder, and with everything in place, I smile and begin.

· · · · · · · · · · · · · · · · MY SCALE · · · · · · · · · · · · · · · ·

My digital scale measures both grams and ounces. I can put an empty pan or bowl on top of it and zero it out after each ingredient is added. Although I will probably remain an "a little of this and a lot of that"–style baker, I enjoy having a scale so my creative adventures at the baking counter can be replicated.

· ·

Extras that are nice to have are:

- a pastry wheel, plain or with fancy wavy edges
- a bench scraper
- a pastry cloth
- cookie cutters to make hearts, leaves, letters, or whatever else might be whimsical or fun to finish off the top of the pie
- a small metal sieve to keep pieces of ice out when you pour chilled water into a glass or cup
- a pastry brush
- a timer for baking
- a scale for exact weighing
- insulated oven mitts to prevent burns when moving pies in and out of the oven
- a wire rack or canning rack for cooling
- a food processor for gluten-free dough

But, never forget the smile, because that is the most important part.

How to Measure

Not all measuring cups are equal. There are different cups for dry measure and for wet measure. The flat edge of a dry measuring cup makes it easy to take a knife and sweep off extra flour so it is level. A wet measuring cup has a spout for pouring and measuring marks on the side. For many years, I've been using dry measuring cups for both dry and wet ingredients, and haven't found this practice to be a deal-breaker. I adjust the amounts and sort of feel my way along. The same is true of measuring spoons. For example, when I dip into the container to measure out tablespoon-size plops of the fat for my dough, and one of my "plops" is a little too big or a tad small, I adjust the next plop as needed. It all seems to work out in the end. Now, let's talk about four ways to measure.

- Sight
- Volume
- Weight
- Taste

SIGHT: I create any new recipe made with fresh or frozen fruit by sight. I put the fruit directly into a pie pan, large or small, until it looks right to my eye. Don't get all worked up about this and fret over what "looking right" means, because deep down you probably

know what is right . . . and if you don't, there are plenty of magazines and baking books that have pictures. For me, "just right" means the fruit is about one half-inch below the rim of the pie pan, especially with juicy fruits like rhubarb, cherries, and berries. Yes, you can go higher than that, but chances are if you do, you'll be setting off your smoke alarm when the filling boils over during the bake and then cleaning the bottom of your oven after it cools. Save the mounding up for mile-high apple pies.

VOLUME: After placing the fruit into the pie pan, I use a measuring cup to scoop the fruit into the mixing bowl. Counting cup by cup, I keep track of how many I put in. Sweetener, seasonings, and thickeners, once added, cannot be removed as easily as fruit can, so I use standard dry measure cups and spoons for them. Although once, when I seasoned some sliced apples with allspice instead of cinnamon, I rinsed them off and started over—but I don't suggest trying this with frozen fruit, or with the likes of fragile blackberries and raspberries, since you'll create a real mess and most likely waste the fruit.

WEIGHT: Weigh the empty pie pan, and then weigh it again with the fruit in it. Now I know the exact weight for the amount of fruit that looks right in my pan in order to write a recipe. I have an OXO digital scale that is great for this.

TASTE: When you have all the ingredients for the filling combined and evenly mixed in the bowl, take a taste. Does it make you want to have another bite? If it does, then it's just right. If not, add a bit more sugar or spice to make it nice, as the nursery rhyme says. Tasting the filling will turn you into a creative and confident pie maker, rather than a by-rote recipe reader. Recipes are merely starting places, and I encourage you to add or subtract ingredients as you go until it pleases you.

SEASONING TIP: Remember you can always add, but it's harder to take away.

Know Your Oven

The best oven is one that has an accurate and even bake, and one would hope that with all the advanced technologies in today's appliance world, this would be an easy order to fill. But when serious pie makers get together, it's not long before you hear, "What do you think of your oven?" It seems that not all ovens are created equal, and finding one that can reliably bake a pie may take some research. Big-name manufacturers and price, whether high or low, won't guarantee that you will get a dream bake. To further confuse things, no two ovens, even if they are identical models, seem to bake alike.

A new oven is a really big-ticket item. Wouldn't it be nice if we could "test drive" models, like we can cars, to see if they live up to the claims printed inside glossy marketing brochures? As for price, the bake of some entry-level apartment-size ovens have given me picture-perfect pies. On the flip side of the coin, I've found wild temperature swings and surprising hot spots in some very high-end models, resulting in pies that could enter the Pie Disaster Hall of Fame. In my experience, despite the claims that a convection oven will more evenly circulate the heat for baking, such ovens—whether with one fan or two—don't always hold up their end of the bargain.

I know it may sound like there are no decent ovens out there. I'm sure that's not the case, but you do need to be diligent about doing your pre-purchase homework when considering the new centerpiece for your baking kitchen. From personal experience, I suggest that you focus especially on the return and repair policy before committing. Recently I bought a used electric range at my local thrift store for $150. It doesn't have a convection bake, a self-clean option, or even an oven light, but what it does have is one of the most even bakes ever, and I consider myself very lucky to have it. It bakes fifty degrees high, so I lower the temperature by that same amount to account for that. Yes, I could have the oven tech come out and adjust it for $100, and some day I just might do that, but until then the five-dollar oven thermometers I bought at the grocery store do just dandy.

Bottom line: If you have an oven with an even bake, you probably already know what a gem it is. Hold on to it, repair it when needed, and pass it on to your children.

Before Oven Thermometers

Before thermostats and preheat lights, there were some hands-on ways to gauge an oven's temperature. *The White House Cookbook* (1898) by Gillette and Ziemann says, "If you can hold your hand in the heated oven while you can count twenty, the oven has just the proper temperature" for baking a pie. I have tried this and found the advice to be accurate. Twenty was as long as I could bear having my hand inside my home oven. Julia Child says, "Great grandmother used to calculate how hot her oven was by the time it took to brown a piece of white paper." In Bee Wilson's fascinating chapter entitled "Measure" from her book, *Consider the Fork*, we learn that in rural parts of Europe, some bakers still use this method.

· · · · · · · · · · · · **OVEN THERMOMETERS** · · · · · · · · · · · · · ·

In pie baking, a difference of 10 degrees may not be large, but a 75-degree difference, high or low, definitely is. An oven thermometer is a great tool to quickly show you how accurately your oven is calibrated. You might even want to have three of them. If two agree, you'll have a pretty fair idea of the real temperature inside. If you find a big disparity between your thermometer and your oven dial, contact a reliable oven repair service to make a house call to re-calibrate it.

· ·

Testing for Hot Spots

Ovens may have hot or cool spots, and it's very easy to test for them. If you have a pie that is browning too slowly, or too quickly, you can use this knowledge to your advantage.

- For each oven you are testing, you will need approximately one loaf of white balloon bread. (Balloon bread is what I call white bread that is super squishy and full of unpronounceable additives.)
- Preheat the oven to 325°F (162°C) for at least 30 minutes.
- On an oven rack, place the bread in even rows with about ½ inch between each piece, covering the rack as completely as possible. Place the rack in the middle of the oven, and close the oven door.
- Set the timer for 25 minutes.
- Open the oven and look to see if the bread is toasted. Add more time in 5-minute increments as needed.
- When some or most of the bread looks like toast, pull the rack out of the oven and set it safely on a counter. Take a look at all pieces on the rack as if they were one big piece of toast. Is it toasted evenly? Are some areas not toasted at all? Are some toasted more than in other places? Where? The sides? Back? Middle?
- Now, turn all pieces over so that you are looking at the bottom side of the toast. What do you see? Is it darker? Is it the same color as the top side? Is the bread toasted evenly? Is some of it not toasted at all? Is some of it toasted more than other places? Where? The sides? Back? Middle?

TIP: If you have a convection oven, do this simple test on both the standard bake and the convection bake settings to have a more complete picture of how your oven performs in each mode.

Rolling Pins and Their Care

To roll out pie dough, all you need is a cylinder and a flat surface. I've rolled out with just about everything over my years of pie making, including wine bottles, water bottles, and rolling pins with or without handles. They all work fine. You may be lucky enough to have in your possession the rolling pin that your great-great-grandmother used. This truly is a family heirloom. Treasure and use it, and then pass it on to the next generation of pie makers along with your family recipes and stories. If you would like to start your own pie lineage with a new pin, visit an independent kitchen store that has a wide selection to find the one that feels just right in your hand. I spent forty-five minutes holding rolling pins, including models that were tapered, straight, with and without handles, made of silicon, metal, and wood, transferring them from hand to hand until only one remained. My choice was a double-ended, tapered, French rolling pin, made from solid rock maple by Fletcher's Mill. I have a baker's dozen of them for use at my workshops. The original off-white color they had when brand-new has mellowed to a rich golden brown with all the dough they have rolled. When I gave my son, Duncan, an accomplished award-winning pie maker in his own right, the option of a brand-new pin or one of my older well-seasoned ones, he chose the older pin and is adding his own rich history to it.

I disregard directions that call for seasoning a new pin with food-grade oil before using. I simply rinse the pin with water, dry well, and put it into service. I never use soap to wash it, but I do wipe it down well with a paper towel before any dough on it has a chance to dry. If dough does dry on it, wrap the pin in a damp towel for 10 to 15 minutes, unwrap, and wipe down the cylinder to easily remove the now-softened dough.

On What to Roll Out Dough

I've rolled out on many surfaces, the oddest being the well-cleaned surface of a neoprene sleeping pad; it was what was available on a camping trip when I was baking pie outside, over and under coals, in a cast-iron Dutch oven. I've been rolling on pastry cloths for many years. I like how the flour sifts down into the weave of the cloth, leaving me with very little extra that I have to brush away.

Here is a more complete list of surfaces I've rolled on. All of them work just fine.

- pastry cloth
- wood
- marble
- Silpat
- Roul'Pat
- wax paper
- plastic wrap
- parchment paper
- the shiny side of freezer wrap

Pastry Cloths

A pastry cloth is a piece of fabric on which one can roll out pie dough. My pastry cloths are made of unbleached cotton denim. I roll out on the smoothest side. Commercially available pastry cloths have neatly hemmed edges, but if you don't mind the fraying strings of unfinished edges, you can cut or even rip a clean piece of heavy cotton fabric and be good to go. Having something between my dough and whatever surface I am rolling on makes stuck dough a thing of the past. In a pinch, you can roll out on a cotton tablecloth, a clean dishtowel, or a pillowcase. A pastry cloth is reusable, which gets big bonus points, too. My favorite cloth has become softer and smoother as I've used it over the years. Each time I lay it on the counter, I think of the family and friends who have received the countless pies I've made when using it.

HOW TO CARE FOR YOUR PASTRY CLOTH

- At the end of your baking session, take a bench scraper or knife and scrape the extra flour off the pastry cloth.
- Shake it to remove even more flour.
- Fold the cleaned-off cloth and place it in a plastic bag in your freezer. It will be chilled and ready for your next pie-making session.
- After about five uses, or if you've spilled something like berry filling on it, wash it on a cold cycle without soap. Add an extra rinse to make sure it is clean.
- Let your pastry cloth air-dry, although sometimes it has found its way into my dryer and it was not the end of the world.

- Some never wash their pastry cloths, and other pie makers do the entire scrape, shake, wash, and dry routine after every session. Whatever pleases you is what you should do.

HOW TO MAKE A DIY PASTRY CLOTH

- Buy ⅔ yard (609 mm) of unbleached or white cotton denim.
- Cut an approximate 20-inch (508-mm) square. Depending on how wide the fabric is, you may have enough material to make a second cloth to give to a friend.
- Fold under a ½-inch (12-mm) edge on all sides and stitch on your machine. If you are feeling fancy, use one of your machine's decorative stitches in a contrasting color thread for a personal touch. If you have a serger, it will trim and finish the edges very quickly. If you are in a big hurry, just cut or rip the cloth to the size you want and neaten the edges up later.

Pie Pans, Plates, and Tins

I have a fairly large collection of pie pans, plates, and tins. I recently counted seventy ceramic pie plates ranging in size from four to ten inches, fourteen Pyrex glass pans from seven to ten inches, and fourteen metal tins from four to twelve inches for a grand total of ninety-eight. This does not include the dozen or so out in the field that may or may not find their way back to my kitchen. I have never found a need to use all the pieces of my collection at once, but I do use each and every one of them.

When asked which material—ceramic, glass, or metal—I like best, it's hard for me to pick just one. If a pie pan works, and most do, I like it. Here are some tips about each.

Glass

If you are a newbie to pie baking, you might want to start with Pyrex. The clear glass will let you see if you've gotten a nicely baked bottom crust. Glass gives an even bake and bakes up more quickly than pottery or ceramic pans.

Ceramic/Pottery

Ceramic pans are inspiring for both new and experienced pie makers. They come in a rainbow of colors to match your kitchen, the season, or your mood. I use all the ceramic makers (Emile Henry, Le Creuset, and Staub) with great results. Staub pans have handles on the

sides, which makes moving a hot pie in and out of the oven very easy. I have Le Creuset's 9-inch deep-dish pans, and a collection of their 5½-inch mini pie pans that are perfect for individual desserts. My 8-inch and 9-inch Emile Henry pans are still going strong after ten years. In fact, all of my ceramic pans are doing exceptionally well. If you are buying older pie pans at an estate or yard sale, the glaze may have lead in it. If there is any question, don't bake in them.

Metal

Bright shiny metal deflects heat, so try not to be swayed by it at the kitchen store. Find a darker pan if possible. I sift through boxes at estate sales, looking for well-loved metal pie tins that are still in useable shape. Some are made with holes that are supposed to help with a crispy bottom crust. I can't say that I've noticed much difference using a "holey" pan, but some pie makers swear by them.

Disposable Aluminum

If you must use a disposable pan for some reason, such as a pie contest where you might not get your beloved Auntie Ruth's heirloom pie pan back (you know, the one she willed you on her death bed), place an aluminum pan inside of a slightly larger Pyrex pan during the bake. The stronger pie pan underneath will give your flexible aluminum pan an even bake as well as a sturdy platform. I once witnessed a beautiful piping-hot apple pie fall to the floor when the flimsy aluminum pan folded in half just as it was being removed from the oven.

Hand-Thrown

If you are considering buying a hand-thrown pie plate for yourself, or to give to a pie maker as a special gift, make sure that the sides and bottom of the pan are all of the same thickness to get an even bake. Ask the potter if the pan is freezer-to-oven-safe and how high and low a temperature it can handle.

Canning Racks for Cooling Racks

After baking a plethora of pies to take to a pie social, I had run out of space on my cooling racks. Looking around for something else I might use, I spied my round metal canning racks sitting on the pantry shelf, and the light bulb went off. Pie makers are a clever breed and can be quite resourceful and inventive when the need arises. I knew that these racks would do quite nicely. Slipping a piping hot pie into the cradle of each, I was able to use their wire handles to move the pies on to a table to cool without even needing pot-holders. I now have seven canning racks that stack away neatly when not being used. You will find them at grocery and hardware stores with good canning sections.

The Big Chill

I cannot emphasize the importance of keeping everything chilled, so bear with me once again while I repeat these words. Keep everything chilled, especially yourself. Here are more hints to help you.

- Keep a mixing bowl and a bag of flour in the freezer.
- Double-bowl your mixing bowl with ice in the lower bowl.
- For a flaky crust, be sure all your fats are well chilled.
- Grate unthawed frozen butter into the dough on hot summer days.
- Handle the dough as little as possible, and roll it out quickly so the fats won't warm up too much.
- At any time, if the fats are melting, stop and pop the pie dough into the freezer for a quick five-minute chill until they firm back up.
- When possible, place your unbaked pie in the fridge while you are preheating the oven, or cover the pie and leave it in the fridge overnight to bake the next day.

On Freezing and Baking Fruit Pies

Pre-making and freezing a fruit pie is another great time saver, especially around the holidays. Instead of putting the pie in the oven, I double wrap it in plastic, label it with the date, and place it on a flat surface in the freezer. When it's time to bake, I simply unwrap it and let it sit on the counter while the oven preheats for fifteen to twenty minutes. Then I give it an egg white or yolk wash (see page 56) with a pastry brush, and pop it in to bake as usual. I look carefully for the signs of the "sizzle-whump" and add some extra time at the end when needed (see Kate's Very Short Glossary of Pie-Making Terms on page 333).

Music to Bake Pie By

There's music playing in my house most of the time, providing a soundtrack for my day. This might have something to do with the fact that my mom taught piano lessons in our living room when I was growing up. These days, the voice of one solitary flute plays as I kindle the morning fire in my woodstove and set the kettle on for tea. By the time it is blazing, the sun is above the horizon and the voices of a string quartet join, while rainbows from prisms hung in east-facing windows dance on my walls. When baking time comes around, there are favorites I've listened to for decades. Joni Mitchell's "Sisotowbell Lane" always puts me in the right frame of mind for making bread, cookies, or pie, and as I set my baking tools out on the wood counter, I sing harmony right along with her without missing a single phrase. My dough-rolling playlist includes Aretha Franklin wailing on "Respect," Joe Cocker belting out "Feeling All Right," and Jefferson Airplane's classic "Embryonic Journey," all of which will date me as having grown up in the 1960s flower-power era. Some say that big-band music, country western, Bach, or even Mahler, complement their baking. Whatever the genre that gets your juices flowing, pick music you absolutely love, turn it up, and sing and dance your heart out. Your pies will love you for it.

Keeping Your Eye on the Pie

Let's remember that we are making pie. It is one simple thing that is divided into two parts: dough and filling. Dough has four ingredients: flour, salt, fat, and water. Filling has four categories, too: fruit, sweetener, seasoning, and thickener. Now, let's proceed.

CHAPTER ONE

Flour, Salt, Fat, and Water

How to Make Pie Dough

In pie making it's important not to overthink the

process and sweat the little stuff. When I make pie dough, it is a reminder for me to keep things simple in my life as well. After a two-and-a-half-year period of being a pie dough fanatic, during which time I tested out recipes on a near-daily basis with ingredients that included national, regional, and local flours; butter, oil, lard, and vegetable shortening; and additions such as cream cheese, or vodka, I found that it takes only four ingredients to make a great dough: flour, salt, fat, and water. These simple ingredients are ones that our great-grandmothers would have recognized. I was astounded when I found my recipe to be nearly identical to the Plain Pastry recipe in *The White House Cookbook* (1898). Some things, like pie, don't change. I like that. It's simple and basic.

Pie is a great teacher. It's helped me find my way, even when it has seemed that everything was falling apart. Pie has taught me how to give up the quest for perfection, although when I have a dough that rolls out perfectly round, with smooth edges, and no rents or tears, I will be the first one to pat myself on the back and say "Look at that beauty!" I used to think this meant I had succeeded—that I had done it "right."

But what about the doughs I make that don't look like the ones on the covers of magazines and in recipe books? Have I failed if they look different? What I have come to realize is that, like life, nothing is the same twice, and rarely is it perfect. I have found ways to "fix" a dough that is falling apart into what I call a "jigsaw puzzle pie"—you know, the one that has a gazillion pieces. I've learned that it's okay to break the rules and in the process find an easier way to get a great result. Being able to patch together dough gave me the confidence to put my own life back together when it had broken apart. Nobody had to see what I went through during those trying times, or at the baking counter either—that was between my dough and me. After piecing together dough that had fallen apart during the rollout stage, only to have the final baked pie grace the cover of a magazine, I realized that perfection is not the goal. Finding beauty and peace through the process is the goal.

Here are the doughs I use for my pies—I invite you to read through them all. If you are new to pie making or haven't made a dough in a while, you will find very detailed directions for making and rolling both traditional pie dough and gluten-free dough, which requires a completely different technique. You'll return to this section to select a dough for the filling recipes that follow in the book. When you find your favorite, it will most likely become known as your dough.

All-Purpose Flour Doughs

Gluten-Free Doughs

Crumbly and Sweet

· · · · · · · · · · · PIE AT ALTITUDE · · · · · · · · · · ·

If you are making pies at high altitude, you may find that your dough needs more liquid and the pie needs a longer baking time depending upon the type of fruit or filling. The source I turn to when baking in rarified air is Susan G. Purdy's book, *Pie in the Sky*.

· ·

How to Make and Roll a Traditional Pie Dough

The recipes for traditional pie doughs are on pages 58 to 63, but I suggest you read this descriptive section before giving it a try.

EQUIPMENT YOU WILL NEED

- A big bowl. It doesn't matter if it is metal, glass, ceramic, or plastic. Make sure it is big enough to get your hands into comfortably. All hand sizes are different, so take that into consideration if you are picking out a bowl to give as a gift. I use a six-quart bowl that fits my hands well and is good for making the dough, as well as being large enough for the filling in an apple pie piled high.
- A knife to chunk up butter, and sharp enough to chop apples and rhubarb.
- A fork. An optional piece of blending equipment. Use your hands if you like. They are your best tools and you will never lose them.
- A vintage vegetable chopper or pastry blender, if you are so inclined.
- A pastry brush.

· · · · · · · · · · **THE PERFECT PASTRY BLENDER** · · · · · · · · ·

Pastry blenders are a source of frustration in my opinion. Who wants cold fat stuck between four or five tines placed way too close together that, furthermore, collapse when you attempt to push them through a brick of butter? Can't someone please make a single blade pastry blender with a comfortable handle, or one with just two strong wide-set tines so the fat can be chopped efficiently without getting stuck? Well, there used to be something just like this, but it was for vegetables—kind of like the original food processor. I find them at antique stores and estate sales, clean them up, and place them right back into service. Butter begins to melt at 59°F (15°C), and these wide-set blades work well, especially on hot days.

· ·

Before you start, remember Pie Making Rule #1: Keep Everything Chilled, Especially Yourself. The first thing I do when beginning a pie-making session is to make a big glass of ice water. I take liberal sips to remind myself to keep calm and cool during the simple process of making dough. Sweaty, hot hands will melt even the coldest of fats, which is the first step to a pie dough disaster, so place your mixing bowl and bag of flour in the freezer. If you look in mine, you'll see bowls, flour, and pastry cloths, plus fats neatly shelved in my fridge, all chilled and ready for a pie-making session at an instant's notice. Keeping my ingredients chilled helps me not worry about the little stuff in pie making . . . or in life.

Flour

I tested my recipes with many local, regional, and national flours; unbleached, all-purpose, and whole grain; and what I like best for pie is unbleached all-purpose white flour. Bob's Red Mill and King Arthur are two brands that consistently give great results. Both are available nationally, and the companies are employee-owned. Bob's is in Portland, Oregon, practically next door to me. If you can't find either brand at your store, use another all-purpose unbleached flour.

Measuring

I don't sift, stir, fluff, or mix the flour. I dip into the cold flour (remember, it came out of the freezer) with a metal cup that I bought at a yard sale for five cents. Chances are, you will have a measuring cup at hand, but my first baking experiences—when I could barely reach the counter—were not all that exact, and my cookies, cakes, and quick breads were good enough to make me want to continue to bake. I've found that a standard-size coffee cup (not mug) measures pretty close to one cup. My favorite has a pretty blue flower pattern on it. My goddaughter Katie gave it to me and I think of her each time I bring it out to use.

Measure 2½ cups (363 grams) of cold flour into the chilled bowl. Exact measuring is needed for cakes, but pie dough—at least mine—is pretty forgiving. A bit extra here or there and it will still turn out fine. If you measure way over or under the rim of your cup, your results may vary from mine. So, use the dip and sweep method and level off the top of the measuring cup with the flat edge of a knife.

Salt

Now put in ½ teaspoon (3 grams) of salt. Use whatever salt you'd like, but don't forget to put it in. I use kosher salt and when once asked why, I replied that if it was good enough for Julia Child, it's good enough for me.

Fat

My favorite butter to use is well-chilled Kerrygold Irish Butter, either the gold (salted) or silver (unsalted) foil-wrapped brick. Kerrygold is European-style butter with higher fat content and less moisture than most paper-wrapped domestic butters. If you can't find European-style butter, use what is available in your area, whether it is foil- or paper-wrapped. Remember that we're making pie and not on a quest for the perfect butter. Butter starts melting at 59°F (15°C), so whatever you use, be sure to keep it well chilled.

Measure out approximately 8 tablespoons of cold butter—4 ounces (112 grams) if you like to use a scale—and chunk it up into eight big pieces with your knife. Place the cold pieces into the bowl on top of the flour.

Now add an equal amount of cold-rendered leaf lard. You are probably wondering what leaf lard is. If you think of the clear fat that is rendered from bacon when you fry it up in the morning, you are halfway there. Leaf lard is fat that also comes from pork, but this special fat comes from a specific area, around the pig's kidneys. Leaf lard is very white and has a slight nutty aroma. It doesn't have the salty flavor that bacon has, although I have heard of some who save their bacon fat for making savory pie dough. Leaf lard was prized by pie makers of generations past, well before the advent of Crisco in the early twentieth century. This old-fashioned fat can be found again at artisan butcher shops and some farmers' markets, or it can be shipped directly to your door (see Sources section on page 338). You can store well-wrapped leaf lard in the fridge for six months and in the freezer for up to one year, although Rose Berenbaum Levy says in *The Pie and Pastry Bible* that two years in the freezer is safe. It's very stable. For more about leaf lard, see page 334. If it works for your diet, I think it is worth the effort to locate, but if not, use any butter, or a combination of butter and vegetable shortening. Whatever you choose, the technique for making the pie dough will be the same, so let's continue.

Dip into the leaf lard container with a tablespoon—or, if you are like me, a soup spoon from the kitchen drawer—and add approximately 8 tablespoons to the butter and flour already in the bowl. If I make one tablespoon big, I make the next smaller. If you use a scale, weigh out 4 ounces (112 grams). Either way, you want to have equal parts butter and leaf lard that add up to about one cup, or 8 ounces (224 grams) of total fat. If you prefer to make all-butter crust, 14 tablespoons, or 7 ounces (196 grams) of chilled butter will do it.

My grandmother swore by "the-stuff-in-the-blue-can-which-shall-remain-nameless." That's what I used to call Crisco, and as I came of age in the 1960s, my "Mother Earth" leanings moved me away from it. You can use equal parts Crisco and butter for a traditional butter and shortening dough (see page 62). It also gives me the best results for my gluten-free vegan pie dough (see page 88), so it has earned a place on my baking shelf.

Water

We'll come back to this ingredient shortly, but before we proceed, take a sip of ice water to remind yourself of Rule #1.

"Smooshing" the Dough

Think good thoughts before you put your hands in the bowl. You might think about the person for whom you are making the pie, something special that has happened, or something wonderful that you would like to have happen in your life.

Make sure your hands are cool, if not downright chilly. If they are hot, dip them into an ice bath for a minute or two, or hold onto ice cubes until you can no longer stand it. Now you have "pastry-maker hands." I believe there is definitely something to the old adage, "Cold hands, warm heart." Be sure to dry your hands before you continue.

Put your cold hands in the bowl, and, as quickly as you can, "smoosh" the fat into the flour before it melts. "Smoosh" is a highly technical term for rubbing the cold fat into the cold flour with your cold hands. Don't dawdle over this, just do it, and then stop before you think you are done. When the flour, salt, and fats appear to be a variety of sizes—ranging from cracker crumbs, peas, almonds, and perhaps one or two small walnut meats—and the entire mess looks incompletely mixed, you are finished. There should be some white floury places as well as all those differently sized fat globules mixed into the dough. It should not look too homogenous.

TIP: If you think a piece of fat is too big, chances are it is. Use some common sense here and quickly break it down into smaller pieces and move on.

Water (Part 2)

For a double-crust pie, recipes generally call for about 8 tablespoons (118 grams) of water, but over my years of pie making, I have had times where it has been anywhere from 5 to 15. There are a lot of variables here. How cold is the flour? How old is the flour? How much were the fats worked? If fat coats the flour too much, it will take less water,

but the dough will be closer to a short pastry—which is still tasty, but denser than the flake pastry we are seeking.

Measure out ½ cup (118 grams) of ice water. I use a small sieve strainer to keep any pieces of ice from falling into the cup, which could cause a "mookie mess" when rolling out the dough (see Kate's Very Short Glossary of Pie-Making Terms on page 333). Evenly sprinkle all the water on top of the flour, salt, and fat while you lightly and quickly move it around in the bowl with a fork or cold fingers. Don't spend a lot of time in there. You are not making cookie dough. Just move the fork, or your fingers, through the dough purposely so that the water has visited all parts of the bowl. This will just take a few seconds.

· · · · · · · · · · · · · ICE WATER AND SIEVES · · · · · · · · · · · ·

If an unseen piece of ice slips into the dough when you are
pouring in cold water, it will melt inside the pastry while
it is chilling in the fridge. When you roll it out, you will
have a big "mookie mess." To avoid a dough-rolling disaster, use a small mesh sieve strainer to filter out any stray
pieces of ice when pouring ice water.

· ·

With a firm handshake, squeeze a handful of dough in your chilly hand to see if it holds together. Just one squeeze, please—if it isn't holding together in one place, it's probably not going to hold together in another place, and if you keep squeezing it all over, you'll just be warming up the fat.

Add one more tablespoon (15 grams) of ice water, and quickly move it through with your fork or fingers. One or two more may be needed, but stop when the dough is slightly moist without feeling like sticky bread dough. When you move the fork around in the bowl and the dough feels a bit sluggish, that's a good clue to stop.

Take your fingers and let them play in the dough for a few seconds, kind of like you are doing hand laundry. With your hands on each side of the dough, push it together firmly into a loaf with one swift movement. From the edge of the dough farthest from you, fold the loaf in half over the top of itself. It's okay if there are pieces falling off, since it won't have come completely together yet. Give the dough a quarter turn, and push it into a loaf again, followed by another fold over itself. I do this push, fold, and turn routine five or six times total to give the dough some extra layers, much like one does for puff pastry. Finally, lift the dough with your hands and form it into a big soft-ball. Some say it feels like cool, moist clay, or even the comforting solidness of patting a baby's bottom. When this is what you feel, stop, put the ball of dough down, and take your hands away. If you keep touching and fussing, you will be over-working and warming up the dough.

Cut the big ball of dough in half. I was a home-schooling mom, so I'll share the short geography lesson I gave my son, Duncan, as we made dough when he was small. "This is our planet Earth. Cut it on the equator into the Northern and Southern Hemispheres. Let's see the magma and striations inside." After it is cut, form each half into a chubby disc about 4 to 5 inches (10 to 12 centimeters) in diameter and 1 ½ to 2 inches (3.5 to 5 centimeters) thick. Wrap each disc tightly in plastic and place them in the fridge to chill for an hour.

Congratulations, you've made dough.

How long will pie dough last?

Pie dough can be left in the fridge for up to four days, but if it has turned hard and dry, there isn't much you can do other than toss it out and make another. Dough made with shortening should be used the day it is made. An all-butter, or a butter and leaf lard dough made with unbleached all-purpose flour, may turn a pale gray when chilled overnight, but will be fine to use. To store dough for longer periods, double-wrap each disc in plastic, date them with a marking pen, pop them into a sealable freezer bag you have also dated, and place them in the freezer. When you are ready to use them, place one or two discs in the fridge to defrost overnight, or place them on the counter for an hour or so. These will defrost faster on a stainless steel counter or a metal baking sheet than on a wood counter or stoneware plate.

There is some difference of opinion as to just how long pie dough will keep in the freezer. In *Baking with Julia*, written by baking legend Dorie Greenspan, I read that dough should be used in one month. The Barefoot Contessa, Ina Garten, in her book, *Make It Ahead*, says three months in the freezer is fine. Julia Child said she once used dough that had been in her freezer for about a year and it seemed to do just fine. I think that if you use frozen dough somewhere between one and three months, it should be okay. If I did find a carefully wrapped disc in the freezer with a 12-month-old date, I probably would use it, hoping that I would get the same results as Julia did.

You can roll dough out immediately after it is made—
when it is at its softest and most pliable—and then chill it.
Roll between two layers of plastic, turning the dough over
and rolling on the opposite side a few times, too. Be sure
to lift the plastic off after every few turns so it won't get
stuck anywhere as you roll. Once the dough is rolled out,
place the entire unit of plastic/dough/plastic onto a baking sheet or cutting board, then let it chill in the fridge.
When you are ready to use your dough, bring it out and let
it temper a bit. Then remove the plastic, place the pastry
in your pan, and continue constructing the pie.

The Gluten Question or Don't Overwork the Dough

Now comes the science part. I promise it will be brief, but keep reading, as this is important. We often hear the words, "Don't overwork the dough." But what, exactly, does that mean? When flour and water are mixed together, they form gluten, a pro-tein. Gluten is your friend in bread dough because it holds the bread together, but gluten is not your friend in pie dough. If we overwork dough by mixing it too much, we will have made a bowlful of strong and connected gluten strands. Under a micro-scope, gluten molecules look like lengths of tightly wound springs, kind of like Shirley Temple curls. Each strand likes to reach out to connect with another strand, which in turn reaches out to connect with another strand, and so on. If we use this very well connected dough for a pie, the end result will be crust that is tenaciously tough, not the flaky crust of our dreams.

So, we return to Rule #1. Work the dough only enough so it holds together and then give it time to chill. We chill for two reasons. Our fats need to be cold and the gluten strands need to relax so they aren't so tense; those tight curls need to look like rolling hills. It will take a minimum of twenty minutes in the refrigerator for the dough, and you, to begin to relax, which is just the right amount of time to make a cup of tea or enjoy a glass of wine. A longer rest of one, two, or more hours, and those gluten strands will be ready to roll.

Techniques and Tricks That Let the Good Pies Roll

Look forward to rolling rather than fearing it. Many pie makers believe that dough can sense fear, and I've worked with enough pastry makers, from beginners to experienced experts, to conclude there is some truth in this. Dough really does want to please you. So if you say, "My dough always falls apart," I can promise you that it will know exactly what to do because you have just given it marching orders. Let's change these words right now to a more positive affirmation, like, "I love my dough. It always rolls out easily for me." Go ahead and say these words out loud, even if you don't believe them yet. You might add, "I know how to fix my dough if it cracks or falls apart, too." With words like these, your dough rolling will become more approachable each time you begin—and remember that practice and patience may not make perfect, but over time you will become the ace pie maker you hope to be. You might even find yourself expanding this kind of positive thought into other areas of your life with good results there, too.

Elbow room is important in dough rolling, so give yourself as much space as you can on the kitchen counter or tabletop. The height of your work surface should be comfortable for you, too. If it is too high, you will be scrunching up your shoulders, in which case a safe stepstool might be needed. If the surface is too low, you may end up with a backache from leaning over, especially if you are rolling out multiple doughs for holiday pies. Be comfortable when you roll your dough, and in all that you do.

In order for the dough not to stick, place something between it and your work surface. You may roll out beautiful dough directly onto a wood or marble surface, but if you cannot lift it into the pie pan, it is not a happy moment. Having something between the dough and the rolling surface makes all the difference between a very frustrating, sticky moment and a more blissful, Zen-like roll-out session, such as Anne Dimock describes in her essay on making pie crust in *Humble Pie*. Most often, I use a homemade pastry cloth.

I spread my pastry cloth on the counter and toss a handful of cold flour into the center from the flour bag that lives in my freezer. It's not necessary to spread out the flour before you set to rolling. The dough will automatically spread out the flour underneath as it is rolled. I'm actually quite a lazy roller, so I let the dough do most of the work for me.

Some pie makers like to pat their dough down to the thickness of about an inch (1.5 centimeters), but I like mine to be approximately one and one-half to two inches (3.5 to 5 centimeters) thick when I start. I call it a "chubby disc." The word "chubby" reminds me of the apple cheeks my son, Duncan, had when he was a toddler. This always brings a smile to my face and puts me in a great frame of mind for rolling dough.

Place the chubby disc on top of the flour and then turn it over so that it has a moderate coating on its top and bottom. Pick up the rolling pin and give a light thwack to the

top of the dough, followed by a few sturdy ones, to assess if it is too hard, too soft, or just right for rolling. If the pressure of a light thwack has left a deep cleft in the dough, then chances are it is too warm, so rewrap it and either pop it in the freezer for around five minutes, or the coldest part of the fridge for ten to fifteen minutes. If the dough breaks apart with the sturdier thwacks, then it is probably too cold and hard. Cover it with plastic wrap and let it warm up, or temper, to a roll-able temperature, which may take up to thirty minutes. In either case, you might enjoy a cup of tea, or chat on the phone with a friend, while you wait. After that interlude the dough will be at a more pliable temperature, one that is just right for rolling. Ideally I like my dough to be between 52 to 54°F (11 to 12°C). The fat will be nicely chilled at that temperature and the dough should roll out well. Above 59°F (15°C), the butter will begin to melt.

I rarely, if ever, roll out dough that is perfectly round. I gave up on that notion a long time ago, and I encourage you to do the same. We are making Pie with a capital "P," and picking up your pin and rolling out dough are merely two steps along the way. Keep your eye on the Pie, and for goodness' sake don't worry about perfect circles and smooth edges. The edges will get cut off anyway, so why spend all that extra energy on something that doesn't matter?

When rolling out dough, we want to make sure that each stroke of the rolling pin begins in the center of the chubby disc but stops about one inch (2.5 centimeters) from the edge. Rolling all the way to or even over the edge of the dough, however, is a sure way to make the edge too thin, causing it to possibly crack and fall apart. Nor should we roll our pin back and forth across the dough as one might do in a pottery class when making the round snake strips for coil pots. The back-and-forth motion will give your dough an identity crisis—it simply won't know whether to get bigger as you roll out towards the edge or smaller as you roll back to the center. So begin in the center of the dough, and using a steady and even pressure, roll out towards the edge without falling off. Pick up the pin, swiftly bring it to the middle of the dough, and roll back towards you without falling off the edge. Turn the dough 90 degrees, and from the center, roll out, lift to the center, and back towards you once again. Continue to turn and roll, always beginning in the center and moving out towards the edges with steady pressure. When the dough is about 8 inches (20 centimeters) in diameter, you can roll out from the middle, like spokes on the wheel of a bicycle. It's okay to flip the dough over, too. Just pick it up as if it were a wet washcloth and turn it over. Suddenly you'll feel that you have an entirely new canvas.

If the dough starts to stick to the pin, wipe it off with your hand or a paper towel, throw a little more flour on top of the dough, and continue. Any spots where the fat looks like it's melting will behave more agreeably with an extra dusting of flour.

Dough must increase in size with each pass of the pin, and like so many things in life, moderation is key. If the dough is not getting larger, then apply a little more pressure with the next roll until you see it grow, but don't press so hard that you squeeze all the air out of it. If the dough is getting too large in just one or two passes of the pin, you may be using too much pressure or it may be too warm, so you will want to lighten up your touch, or possibly pop it into the freezer for a few moments. Every dough you make will feel ever so slightly different, and with practice you'll learn how much or how little pressure to apply as you find its sweet spot.

Once you have rolled your dough one to two inches (2.5 to 5 centimeters) larger than the size of the pie pan you have chosen to use, it is time to transfer it into the pan. This is not hard. Place the rolling pin in the center of the dough so that the long side of the pin faces one of the corners of the pastry cloth (or whatever you have chosen to place between your dough and rolling surface). Slide the left palm of your hand under the pastry cloth. Place the palm and fingers of your right hand lightly on the top of the dough and move both hands together as you lift and drape the pastry cloth over the pin so that the two edges of the cloth meet. Pull your hands away and fold back the cloth to find your dough resting and folded over the rolling pin. Adjust as necessary so that the dough is evenly distributed.

Remove any extra flour sitting on top of the dough with a pastry brush. This is not prima donna brushing. Just quickly and gently sweep it off. Then carefully lift the pin a bit so you can brush any extra flour off the backside of the dough. Don't hold the pin up too high, as the weight of the dough could cause it to tear, but let it rest partially on the rolling surface as you brush. After brushing, gently place the dough-draped pin across the center of the pie pan, and with great aplomb, roll the pin across to the side of the pan that just a moment before was empty. A word of caution here: If you roll too fast, the dough may end up on the counter or even the floor, but if you roll too slowly, the dough may break. Again, moderation is the key to success. I like the image of being at a stop-light. When it turns green, you don't want to push down on the gas pedal like a racecar driver and spin out, nor do you want to go so slow that it takes two minutes to cross the intersection. Roll out confidently, as if you do this every day, and for goodness' sake, don't let your dough know that you have any fear. As Julia Child said, "You are the boss of that dough." Adjust as needed so the dough is more or less centered. Then let its natural weight ease down into the pan as if you were covering a sleeping baby. There is no need to stretch the dough. In fact, if you do, it will stretch back as it bakes, since pie dough has a memory.

If either you or your dough feel spent at this point, cover it with plastic wrap and place it in the fridge while you have a sip of ice water (or something stronger). It's absolutely fine and highly recommended for you both to have a little chill time. This will allow the fats to firm back up and the inevitable gluten strands you have created to relax.

To roll gluten-free dough, skip ahead to page 72.

· · · · · · · · · · · · · ON FREEZING DOUGH · · · · · · · · · · · · ·

Place a single rolled-out dough on top of a large plastic wrapped cookie sheet. Cover the dough with another large sheet of plastic wrap. Continue in this manner as you roll, cover, and stack additional doughs on top of the first. Wrap the entire lot well in plastic wrap, and pop into the freezer. Bring one or two doughs out to warm up on the counter while making a filling. This is a great time-saver if you have a last-minute call for pie.

You can also freeze an unbaked, dough-filled pie pan that is double wrapped in plastic. While preheating your oven, set the unfilled, frozen shell on the counter while you make the filling. Add your filling to the shell and place the pie in the oven to bake. Dough that is frozen will have less shrinkage, too.

PLEASE USE COMMON SENSE WHEN BAKING WITH PIE PANS STRAIGHT FROM THE FREEZER! If you have a beautiful heirloom or expensive pottery pie pan, do not risk its loss with wild temperature swings from freezer to oven. Against manufacturer recommendations but in the name of research, I placed a glass pan filled with a solidly frozen pie directly in a preheated oven only to have it explode. To avoid this, I let a frozen pie sit on the counter for at least fifteen minutes before popping it in the oven. Of course, you won't have this problem if you are baking frozen pies in disposable aluminum.

· ·

A Pie Maker's Signature: Vents, Appliqués, Crimps, Flutes, Lattice

Each pie maker will finish a pie in a way that identifies it as his or her own—a signature, if you will. I don't always save the flutes and scallops for special occasions like weddings and birthdays, because every day is one worth celebrating. Here are some suggestions for vents and finishes for you to try after you have rolled the edges of the pie pastry up (or under, as some do).

Vents

My own signature vents are three large commas in the middle of the top crust that fan out evenly from a center point, plus five little Vs spaced around the edges of the pie. On my gluten-free pies, I cut a vent hole about the size of a silver dollar right in the middle of the top crust. Some cut vents in the shape of the fruit that is in the filling—apples or cherries with leaves are always a favorite—and I've seen some beautiful shafts of wheat decorating top crusts, too. The only rule is that the vents should go all the way through the top crust but not as far as the bottom crust. A break in the bottom crust can cause the fruit filling to leak through, which will cause slices to stick in the pan when you are trying to dish them up.

Appliqués

A fun technique is to cut out pieces of dough with cookie cutters and appliqué them on. These shapes are easily "glued" on to the top of the unbaked pie with a drop of water, or whatever wash you are using (see page 56). Pippi Konstanski, artist and pie maker, creates pies that are beautiful, whimsical, and most often have a message on top, such as "Beauty is in the pie of the beholder" or "You are the apple of my pie." She uses alphabet, heart, and bird cookie cutters that have been in her family for many years. After rolling out well-chilled dough, she cuts out her complete design, and arranges it on the top crust of the pie just before it goes into the oven. Multiple cutouts can also go directly on top of a fruit filling, a clever variation on a lattice theme. I have been collecting cookie cutters since Duncan was a little boy and look forward to passing them on to him someday. To decorate a custard pie, bake cut outs separately on a baking sheet for 5 to 7 minutes, cool, and place on top of the baked and cooled pie.

Crimps

My grandmother folded the top crust over and used a simple fork to crimp and seal in the filling. Most often, I finish my pies this way as I think of early morning pie-making sessions with her in the kitchen. When you are using the fork to crimp, try not to pierce the body of the pie unless you want a few extra vents on the side.

Scallops

Pinch the pastry with your thumb and index finger all around the rim, and finish by lightly pressing a fork, or your finger, between the scallops to flatten and secure the pastry on top of the pie pan.

Rope

Position your little finger on top of the edge and at an angle slightly away from the rim of the pie pan. Press down at the same angle at even intervals as you rotate the pie pan.

Flutes

Gently wiggle your index finger underneath the edge of dough and lift it up from the pie pan slightly. With two fingers of the opposite hand, surround the lifted dough and press firmly on to the edge of the pan.

Braids

Cut three long strips, each about ½ inch (1.25 centimeters) wide or less from trimmings you have re-rolled and braid them together. Splice lengths together with a drop of water to make the strips longer. Paint a little water on the edge, and lay the braid around the circumference of the pie, tucking in the ends. Press down lightly all the way around the braid to be sure it stays. This works best in a chilly kitchen, with cool hands and well-chilled dough. If the fats start to melt, place your work in the fridge or freezer for a few minutes and continue when it feels firmer.

How to Weave A Lattice Top

Lattice tops can seem challenging to new pie makers. Let me share with you a technique that I believe will demystify the process, and you will make a woven lattice-top show-stopper. Always work from left to right, folding or unfolding only one strip at a time.

- First, roll out a disc of dough and cut ten strips that are about 1 inch (2.5 centimeters) wide and 2 inches (5 centimeters) longer than the width of your pie pan.
- Evenly lay five strips vertically across the top of the pie and fold up strips two and four (the even-numbered strips) halfway.
- Take one of your remaining strips and lay it horizontally over the three odd-numbered strips in the middle of the pie.

Now the fun begins—and all you have to remember is to go methodically from left to right without skipping a strip, all the while saying these words: "If it's down it goes up; if it's up it goes down." Here we go. Starting with the far left strip, which we will call #1, you are going to weave:

- Strip #1 is down, so fold it up over the crosswise strip.
- Strip #2 is up, so unfold it down over the crosswise strip.
- Strip #3 is down, so fold it up over the crosswise strip.
- Strip #4 is up, so unfold it down over the crosswise strip.
- Strip #5 is down, so fold it up over the crosswise strip.
- Take one of your remaining strips and lay it horizontally, covering the two even-numbered down strips closest to you.

So far, so good. Let's keep going, but remember not to get ahead of yourself. Starting again on the left-hand side:

- Strip #1 is up, so unfold it down over the crosswise strip.
- Strip #2 is down, so fold it up over the crosswise strip.
- Strip #3 is up, so unfold it down over the crosswise strip.
- Strip #4 is down, so fold it up over the crosswise strip.
- Strip #5 is up, so unfold it down over the crosswise strip.
- Take one of your remaining strips and lay it horizontally, covering the three odd-numbered strips closest to you. Unfold the two even strips over it.

You're halfway there. Let's go on:

- Turn the pie 180 degrees around, and fold the odd-numbered strips up over the horizontal strip.
- Take one of your remaining strips and lay it horizontally over the two even-numbered strips closest to you.

Repeat your mantra—"If it's down it goes up; if it's up it goes down."—and do the up/down thing all the way through strip #5. Strip #1 on the left will be up when you start. Ready?

- Strip #1 is up, so unfold it down over the crosswise strip.
- Strip #2 is down, so fold it up over the crosswise strip.
- Strip #3 is up, so unfold it down over the crosswise strip.
- Strip #4 is down, so fold it up over the crosswise strip.
- Strip #5 is up, so unfold it down over the crosswise strip.
- Place the last strip horizontally over the three odd strips.
- Flip the two even-numbered strips down and over the horizontal strip and you're done.

You should have a full lattice weave on top. Give yourself a pat on the back and know that I am so proud of you. You can do this with any number of strips. Make them wide or narrow or even a combination of the two so it looks like a tartan plaid. With practice you'll be ready to teach someone else.

EASY VARIATION: Cut ten strips. Lay five strips horizontally on top of the pie. Lay the remaining five strips on top in a vertical direction. The pie will still be wonderful whether it has a true woven top or not.

Washes and Glazes

Each wash or glaze will give a slightly different look to the top of the pie.

- An egg white and water wash used with traditional all-purpose flour dough results in a nice shine on the top of fruit pies.
- An egg yolk and water wash on gluten-free dough creates a more golden appearance.
- A full egg and water wash creates a rich color on top of a savory pie.
- You can also brush on a glaze of milk, including almond, hemp, soy, rice, cow, or even goat. They all work.

Traditional *Art of the Pie* Leaf Lard and Butter Dough

This is the dough I teach to pie makers across the country and abroad. I use it on a daily basis for sweet and savory pies, quiches, tarts, crostatas, hand pies, and pie pops. Add a tablespoon or two of sugar to the dry ingredients if you wish to make it slightly sweet. For more detailed instructions on rolling out the dough, see pages 42 to 49.

FOR ONE DOUBLE-CRUST PIE OR TWO SINGLE-CRUST PIES

INGREDIENTS
· · · · ·

2½ cups (363 grams) all-purpose flour, unbleached (use dip and sweep method on page 36)

½ teaspoon (3 grams) salt

8 tablespoons (112 grams) salted or unsalted butter, cut into tablespoon-size pieces

8 tablespoons (112 grams) rendered leaf lard, cut into tablespoon-size pieces

½ cup (118 grams) ice water + 1–2 tablespoons (15–30 grams) more as needed

Additional flour for rolling out dough

· · · · · · · · · · · · · · · · · · **NOTES** · · · · · · · · · · · · · · · · · ·

Leaf lard is available at some butcher shops, farmers' markets, and also by mail order. Be sure to use rendered leaf lard. (Read more about leaf lard on page 334.)

Chill the dough on the lowest and coldest shelf in your fridge. After chilling, dough discs may be frozen for one to three months.

· ·

PROCEDURE

· · · · ·

1. Put all ingredients but the ice water in a large bowl.
2. With clean hands, quickly smoosh the mixture together, or use a pastry blender with an up and down motion, until the ingredients look like cracker crumbs with lumps the size of peas and almonds. These lumps will make your crust flaky.
3. Sprinkle ice water over the mixture and stir lightly with a fork.
4. Squeeze a handful of dough to see if it holds together. Mix in more water as needed.
5. Divide the dough in half and make two chubby discs about 5 inches (12 centimeters) across.
6. Wrap the discs separately in plastic wrap, and chill for about an hour.

ROLLING INSTRUCTIONS

· · · · ·

1. Take out the dough discs and let them temper until they feel slightly soft to the touch and easy to roll out. Unwrap one disc and place it on a well-floured board, pastry cloth, parchment paper, or plastic wrap.
2. Sprinkle some flour onto the top of the disc. Thump the disc with your rolling pin several times. Turn it over and thump the other side.
3. Sprinkle more flour onto the top of the dough as needed to keep the pin from sticking, and roll the crust out from the center in all directions.
4. When the dough is 1 to 2 inches (3 to 5 centimeters) larger than your pie pan, brush off the extra flour on both sides.
5. Fold the dough over the top of the pin and lay it in the pie pan carefully.
6. Don't worry if the crust needs to be patched together. Paint a little water where it needs to be patched and "glue" on the patch piece.
7. Put the filling in the pie and repeat the process with the other disc.

MAKING TRADITIONAL DOUGH IN A FOOD PROCESSOR

Yes, traditional dough can be made in a food processor. Here's how to do it:

1. Chill the work bowl and blade.
2. Put flour, salt, and fat into the chilled work bowl just as you would if doing it by hand.
3. Pulse 15 times.
4. Add 4 tablespoons of ice water.
5. Pulse 10 more times.
6. Add 4 more tablespoons of ice water.
7. Pulse 5 more times.
8. Turn the ingredients into a bowl, add more ice water as needed, and finish off by hand.

Traditional *Art of the Pie* All-Butter Dough

An all-butter crust is not as flaky as a butter and leaf lard crust, but the flavor can't be beat.

FOR ONE DOUBLE-CRUST PIE OR TWO SINGLE-CRUST PIES

INGREDIENTS
· · · · ·

2½ cups (363 grams) all-purpose flour, unbleached (use dip and sweep method on page 36)

½ teaspoon (3 grams) salt

14 tablespoons (196 grams) salted or unsalted butter, cut into tablespoon-size pieces

½ cup (118 grams) ice water + 1–2 tablespoons (15–30 grams) more as needed

Additional flour for rolling out dough

PROCEDURE
· · · · ·

1. Put all ingredients but the ice water in a large bowl.
2. With clean hands, quickly smoosh the mixture together, or use a pastry blender with an up and down motion, until the ingredients look like cracker crumbs with lumps the size of peas and almonds. These lumps will make your crust flaky.
3. Sprinkle ice water over the mixture and stir lightly with a fork.
4. Squeeze a handful of dough to see if it holds together. Mix in more water as needed.
5. Divide the dough in half and make two chubby discs about 5 inches (12 centimeters) across.
6. Wrap the discs separately in plastic wrap, and chill for about an hour.
7. See page 59 for rolling instructions.

Traditional *Art of the Pie* Butter and Shortening Dough

If you're not using leaf lard, this recipe, made with butter and vegetable shortening, works best the day it is made.

FOR ONE DOUBLE-CRUST PIE OR TWO SINGLE-CRUST PIES

INGREDIENTS
· · · · ·

2½ cups (363 grams) all-purpose flour, unbleached (use dip and sweep method on page 36)

½ teaspoon (3 grams) salt

8 tablespoons (112 grams) salted or unsalted butter, cut into tablespoon-size pieces

8 tablespoons (112 grams) vegetable shortening

½ cup (118 grams) ice water plus 1–2 tablespoons (15–30 grams) more as needed

Additional flour for rolling out dough

PROCEDURE
· · · · ·

1. Put all ingredients but the ice water in a large bowl.
2. With clean hands, quickly smoosh the mixture together, or use a pastry blender with an up and down motion, until the ingredients look like cracker crumbs with lumps the size of peas and almonds.
3. Sprinkle ice water over the mixture and stir lightly with a fork.
4. Squeeze a handful of dough to see if it holds together. Mix in more water as needed.
5. Divide the dough in half and make two chubby discs about 5 inches (12 centimeters) across.
6. Wrap the discs separately in plastic wrap and chill for an hour.
7. See page 59 for rolling instructions.

Traditional *Art of the Pie* Cheddar Cheese Dough

This dough provides a great variation when paired with The Quintessential Apple Pie (see page 151), and is scrumptious with Sausage and Apple Pie (see page 311). After I grate up the sharp cheddar cheese, I turn it onto a cutting board and chop it up more finely with a knife.

FOR ONE DOUBLE-CRUST PIE OR TWO SINGLE-CRUST PIES

INGREDIENTS
· · · · ·

2½ cups (363 grams) all-purpose flour, unbleached (use dip and sweep method on page 36)

½ teaspoon (3 grams) salt

¼ pound (115 grams) Kerrygold Dubliner Cheese or other sharp cheddar cheese, grated and chopped fine with a knife (about 1 cup grated)

8 tablespoons (112 grams) salted or unsalted butter, cut into tablespoon-size pieces

6–8 tablespoons (88–118 grams) ice water

Additional flour for rolling out dough

PROCEDURE
· · · · ·

1. Combine all ingredients but the ice water in a large bowl. With clean hands or a pastry cutter, blend the mixture together until it looks like coarse meal with some lumps in it.
2. Sprinkle ice water over the mixture and stir lightly with a fork.
3. Squeeze a handful of dough together. Mix in a bit more water as needed.
4. Divide the dough in half and make two chubby discs about 5 inches (12 centimeters) across. Wrap the discs separately in plastic wrap and chill for an hour.
5. See page 59 for rolling instructions.

English Hot Water Pastry

Here's the hot water crust used for Traditional English Pork Pies (see page 323) that I learned to make at the School of Artisan Food in Nottinghamshire. Gluten-free flour does not work with this pastry so be sure to use all-purpose flour and bread flour.

MAKES ENOUGH PASTRY FOR TWO PORK PIES

INGREDIENTS
· · · · ·

1½ cups (336 grams) rendered leaf lard

1 cup (236 grams) boiling water

1 tablespoon (9 grams) salt

4 cups flour (about half bread flour [304 grams] and half all-purpose flour [290 grams])

Additional flour for rolling out dough

PROCEDURE
· · · · ·

1. Melt the lard and let it cool but not harden.
2. Carefully pour boiling water into the melted lard. Add salt and stir.
3. Pour the mixture over the flour and mix quickly with a knife or wooden spoon. As soon as possible with your hands, knead briefly until it is well mixed, and shape into 2 balls. Cover the balls in plastic and let them cool until they are about 75 to 80°F (23 to 26°C).
4. Flour the work surface and roll the balls out to a rectangle about ¼-inch (.6 centimeter) thick. Fold the dough in and on to itself by thirds. Repeat the roll and fold one more time. Let the dough rest and cool for about 20 minutes until it is room temperature, but still quite pliable. Once the dough is finished, continue on to make English Pork Pies (see page 323).

Enlightened Pie Dough

When writing her second cookbook, Kim O'Donnel was searching for pie dough that would use less animal fat and asked if I might be able to come up with something that fit the bill. With some ideas percolating in my head, I suggested we make a hot water crust using a combination of butter and olive oil, and use a French "letter" fold technique used for puff pastry. The result was dough with flaky layers that Kim called "a revelation." Note that this dough has a much shorter chill time.

FOR ONE DOUBLE-CRUST PIE OR TWO SINGLE-CRUST PIES

INGREDIENTS
. . . . .

3 cups (435 grams) all-purpose flour, unbleached (use dip and sweep method on page 36)

¼ teaspoon plus ⅛ teaspoon (1.5 grams) salt

¼ teaspoon plus ⅛ teaspoon (2.5 grams) baking powder

6 tablespoons (170 grams) cold unsalted butter

½ cup (96 grams) water

6 tablespoons (84 grams) olive oil

Additional flour for rolling out dough

PROCEDURE
. . . . .

1. While measuring the flour, remove 1½ tablespoons to be saved and used for rolling out the dough. Place the remaining flour, salt, and baking powder in a small mixing bowl, wrap with plastic, and chill for about 10 minutes.

2. Transfer the flour mixture into the bowl of a food processor and pulse a few times just to mix. Slice the butter into 6 pieces and add

to the food processor. Using the "pulse" function, mix briefly until the mixture looks and feels like fluffy sand.

3. Place the water in a small saucepan and heat until nearly boiling. Measure out 6 tablespoons of the water and transfer to a small bowl. Add the olive oil and whisk to mix.

4. Pour the oil-water mixture on top of the flour mixture and pulse until the dough just comes together. It may pull away slightly from the sides of the bowl. The dough should feel soft, warm, and pliable, not hard and crumbly.

5. Place a pastry cloth, silicone mat, or sheet of parchment paper on top of a flat surface, and set the dough on top. Sprinkle some of the extra flour on the top and bottom of the dough. Surround the dough with both hands and mold it into a thick lump.

6. Roll the dough in quick, even strokes, making a quarter turn after every few strokes. Check regularly to make sure the dough is not sticking. (A dough scraper is helpful at this stage.) Roll to an approximate 9- to 10-inch (23 to 25 centimeters) rectangle. If the edges aren't perfect, don't worry.

7. Fold the dough in and onto itself by thirds. Your dough will look like a small notebook. Make a quarter turn, then roll out the dough into a new rectangle, which will likely be smaller. Fold the dough in and onto itself by thirds one more time so that it is about a 4- to 5-inch (10 to 12 centimeters) square packet. Roll lightly on top to seal the layers.

8. Cut the dough into 2 halves, wrap the halves in plastic, and allow them to rest in the refrigerator for 10 to 12 minutes. Roll the dough when it is about body temperature.

Jennifer's Fried Pie Dough

Jennifer makes mighty fine fried pies with dough that is tender and forgiving. The texture is closer to biscuit dough and the lard makes it easy to work. You'll need to use gluten-full flours on this one. See page 138 for directions on making and frying the pies.

ENOUGH DOUGH FOR ONE DOZEN FRIED PIES

INGREDIENTS
. . . . .

2 cups (290 grams) all-purpose flour, unbleached (use dip and sweep method on page 36)

½ teaspoon (3 grams) salt

8 tablespoons (112 grams) rendered leaf lard

½ cup (115 grams) cold whole milk or half-and-half

Additional flour for rolling out dough

PROCEDURE
. . . . .

1. Sift the flour and salt together.
2. Mix in the cold lard with your fingertips until the mixture resembles sand.
3. Stir in the milk until the dough looks shaggy and is just holding together.
4. Turn the dough onto a floured board and gather it together into a ball, then flatten into a disc and cut into quarters.
5. Cut the quarters into thirds and form them into small balls. Cover the balls and use as needed.

The day your beloved child heads off to their

freshman year of college is a memorable one. Duncan had chosen a school four hours and a ferry ride from our home, and on the appointed day we loaded up the "pie-mobile" with all the essentials this young man would need—clothes, computer, stereo, and skateboard—to head across the water for the move to university life.

Feeling both happy and sad about this major milestone, I took a walk on the beautiful campus. My reverie was interrupted by an unexpected call from my doctor. Doctors don't usually call on weekends . . . unless there is something wrong. I stopped and listened as she informed me that, based on the results of recent tests, I had celiac disease. Celiac is a condition where the small intestine is hypersensitive to gluten—you know, the stuff in pie dough.

Gluten is a way of life for bakers. We live and breathe flour. It coats our clothes, our counters, our hands, and many times the inside of our homes. Opening a new bag of flour is a promise of something delicious to come, and there is nothing I like better than putting my hands in a bowl full of soft sticky bread dough to knead it until it becomes perfectly silky and smooth. Then there is that glorious slice from a just-baked loaf, still hot from the oven and topped with a slathering of melting butter. My ultimate comfort food was no longer to be mine? Knowing that some of my gluten-free friends with severe sensitivities couldn't even be in the same room with flour, I was already thinking of the candles I would need to light to Vesta, the goddess of the hearth, praying that this would not

be so with me. I began to rattle off questions to my doctor. "Does this mean I can no longer bake?" "Will I still be able to make pie?" "What do I eat now?" "What do I do now?" Her three-word order was simple and direct. "Stop. Eating. Gluten." This shook me to my baker's core, even though she assured me that I would lose the gluten craving in four days' time. But eating it again? "Never. No way. Not possible." We set up a time to meet the following week so she could go over more guidelines to help me adjust to my new gluten-free lifestyle. As I drove home, there was much to think about.

My diet was a healthy one with lots of legumes, fruit, greens, meat, fish, and fowl. When I stopped eating gluten I started to feel a lot better, and have never turned back. And my pie making? The entire process from start to finish had become a daily ritual that I dearly loved and looked forward to. What to do but turn the page to begin a new chapter, and learn to make the best gluten-free pie I possibly could.

My purpose was twofold: pie for me, and pie for those like me, who no longer could enjoy a crust made with all-purpose flour. Using different gluten-free starch and flour combinations, I tried some of my standard recipes. Having little experience with this kind of baking, my first attempts at gluten-free dough were mediocre at best. I found the dough frustratingly hard to handle and it required lots of patching during rolling. Many trials ended up in the compost because the texture seemed closer to cardboard after baking. There were very few gluten-free flour mixes on the market at that time, and I tried them all. None had the great flavor or the "wow factor" I sought, and it became clear to me that to make a good gluten-free piecrust I would need to explore alternative ingredients, as well as learn and create new techniques. Wanting no one to be pie deprived, my new goal became pie for everyone—whether gluten-full or gluten-free.

The experiments to create a viable gluten-free flour blend were on. One session began with a lineup of ten bags of gluten-free flours and starches set in front of me. I closed my eyes, reached my hands into each bag, and put a little of this and a lot of that into a bowl until I had something that approached the texture and feel of an all-purpose flour. The finished baked result was disastrous and totally inedible in both texture and taste. I headed back to the baking counter to try again and again, always hoping for better results. I regularly heard, "Well, for a gluten-free pie, it's not bad." Not remotely close to my goal of a pie that could stand on its own merits, gluten-free or not.

I finally had a breakthrough with a homemade concoction of seven flours and starches, but with so many ingredients just for the flour mix, it seemed a lot to deal with before making dough. I spent another year experimenting and refining off and on, until I had streamlined the mix to just four ingredients: one part each of cornstarch, sweet white rice flour, tapioca flour, and one-half part potato starch. Using this mix my gluten-free dough results were consistently good and the combination has become the go-to, all-purpose gluten-free flour mix I use with all my sweet or savory fillings.

The technique required to make gluten-free pie is completely different from how I make gluten-full pie. The advice I will share with you, which I wish I had known at the beginning, is this: to successfully make a gluten-free pie, forget everything you know about traditional gluten-full pie making. For example, I make gluten-full dough by hand, but my gluten-free dough is made in a food processor. Once the gluten-free dough is made, I do not touch it unless there is a layer of plastic wrap between the dough and my hands at all times. One of the great advantages in gluten-free pie making is that, since there is no gluten in the dough, it can be re-rolled without any fear of it becoming tough due to overworking. If the fats have become too warm at any time, gather the dough back into a ball, rewrap it in plastic, and return it to the fridge to re-chill. You can re-roll when the fats have chilled again, and re-chill and roll more than once if necessary. Very cool!

Gluten-Free Dough and How to Roll It

The recipes for gluten-free dough are on pages 78 to 92, but I suggest you read this more descriptive section on making, rolling, and finishing before giving it a try. It is not necessary to add gums to this dough.

1. Into the work bowl of a food processor place Gluten-Free Flour Mix (page 79), salt, butter, leaf lard, or another fat of your choice, like shortening. Pulse with a metal blade about ten times to chop up the fat into irregular pieces. Add eggs and vinegar (add sugar if you are making a sweet dough). Pulse again until it all comes together. Have some ice water ready in case you need to add a bit more. The dough will feel much softer than traditional gluten-full pie dough.

2. Turn this big blob of dough onto a large sheet of plastic wrap and securely wrap it. It will be the size of a big softball. Dough can also be divided in half and wrapped. Place in the fridge for approximately two hours or in the freezer for twenty minutes until it is very well chilled.

Rolling Gluten-Free Dough

1. Plastic wrap works better than wax paper or anything else I've tried with this dough. Piecing together cheap plastic wrap is not the best because the two pieces inevitably come apart when rolling. Use wrap that is heavier and wider. Spread out a big sheet of plastic wrap and sprinkle some Gluten-Free Flour Mix on top. Cut the ball of chilled dough into two discs and set one on top of the floured plastic wrap. Sprinkle some additional gluten-free flour on top. Finally, place a second large sheet of plastic wrap on top of the flour-covered dough. You've made a dough sandwich and are ready to move on to rolling.

2. To roll gluten-free dough, I use a double handled straight rolling pin like the one my grandmother, Geeg, used. With this dough, it doesn't matter how you go about rolling, so back and forth, out from the middle to the edges, or even around in a circle, will work. Occasionally flip the sandwich over. When you do, carefully lift the plastic wrap off and place it back down on the top of the dough lightly. This makes it easier to remove the wrap from the dough later when it is completely rolled out. Roll the dough one to two inches (2.5 to 5 centimeters) larger than your pie pan, and to a thickness of ¼ to ⅓ inch (a bit less than 1 centimeter). This will be thicker than the ⅛-inch usually recommended for gluten-full dough. Through

trial and error I have found gluten-free dough is much easier to work with when thicker. At any time if the fat in the dough feels like it is too soft or melting, slide a rimless cookie sheet underneath the whole works, and pop it into the freezer for a few minutes.

Transferring Gluten-Free Dough to the Pie Pan

The technique for transferring gluten-free dough to the pie pan is different from that of gluten-full dough. It's not hard, it's just different. These are very specific instructions, but if you follow them, soon the process will become second nature to you. A quick chill before you are ready to transfer the dough to the pie pan is helpful, especially for the first few times, until you get the hang of this technique.

1. For the first step, keep all the layers of plastic on the "dough sandwich," and switch to a French double-ended tapered pin, if you have one, or even a dowel. Lightly set the pin on the upper layer of the plastic wrap "sandwich," and gently fold all layers, including plastic wrap, over the pin until the edges meet. It will look like the shape of half a pie. The layer of plastic that is facing you was once the bottom of the sandwich. Now it is the uppermost layer of the sandwich. Lift up the pin and begin to pull off the plastic wrap facing you with quick little tugs while making a "tchoo-tchoo-tchoo" sound until the first layer of plastic is completely removed. A long and fast pull may cause this more fragile dough to rip, and the sound you would make is something like "tchooooooooooooo . . . OOPS!" Once that first layer of plastic is off, you will have dough on the outside and a remaining layer of plastic wrap on the inside still touching the pin.

2. Lightly place the dough-covered pin on top of the middle of the pie pan rim. With your fingers, hold the edge of the uppermost piece of plastic wrap that remains in the middle of the "filling" section of the "sandwich," and carefully help it across to the other side of the pie pan. The dough will now cover the entire pie pan with a layer of plastic wrap on top of it. Do not remove the plastic wrap yet, but pat and adjust the dough as necessary with it still covering the dough. If the dough feels "soft" at any time, back it goes into the fridge or freezer until the fats have chilled. You can continue when it feels more solid and workable.

Finishing Gluten-Free Edges

1. **FOR A SINGLE-CRUST GLUTEN-FREE PIE:** With plastic wrap covering the edge, carefully crimp or finish as desired. Then, making the "tchoo-tchoo-tchoo" sound, remove the plastic wrap with quick little tugs. Remember that big tugs may cause big tears. Place your filling into the unbaked shell, and place it in the fridge or freezer to chill while you preheat the oven.

2. **FOR A DOUBLE-CRUST GLUTEN-FREE PIE:** Roll out the upper crust and leave the plastic wrap on top while you carefully place it on top of the filling. Then crimp or flute the edges as above. The "tchoo-tchoo-tchoo" sound will help you to make quick little tugs when removing the plastic wrap from the gluten-free dough.

3. Make any last adjustments on the edges with a small piece of plastic wrap covering your fingers.

Venting and Chilling

Narrow vents often bake themselves back together in gluten-free dough, so I cut a vent hole about the size of a half dollar in the middle of the pie to let out the steam during the bake time. This also makes it easy to identify the pie as being gluten-free when serving both gluten-free and gluten-full pies. Finally, drape the plastic wrap loosely over the top of the pie and place it in the fridge for a final chill before baking. I've left pies in my refrigerator overnight and baked them the next day with very good results. Freezing gluten-free pies up to a month and baking them without defrosting works well, too.

· · · · · · · · · · · · · · · · · NOTE · · · · · · · · · · · · · · · · ·

I use an egg yolk wash on my gluten-free pies to add color. The gluten-free dough recipes include this as an ingredient, and you can swap the egg white wash for the egg yolk wash in pie recipes where you're using gluten-free crust in place of gluten-full.

· ·

Gluten-Free
Leaf Lard and Butter Dough

The technique for making and rolling this dough is very different from gluten-full dough. Use a food processor to make it. You will have a layer of plastic wrap between you and the dough at all times. I suggest that you read through the directions (on pages 72 to 76) for making and rolling out gluten-free dough several times before trying your hand at it. Leave the sugar out if you are making a savory pie.

FOR ONE DOUBLE-CRUST PIE OR TWO SINGLE-CRUST PIES

INGREDIENTS
· · · · ·

2½ cups (396 grams) Kate's Gluten-Free Flour Mix (recipe follows)

½ teaspoon (3 grams) salt

1 tablespoon (12 grams) sugar (optional)

8 tablespoons (112 grams) salted or unsalted butter, cut into
    tablespoon-size pieces

8 tablespoons (112 grams) rendered leaf lard, cut into
    tablespoon-size pieces

2 large eggs, fork-beaten

1 tablespoon (15 grams) apple cider vinegar (Bragg's or another
    artisan apple cider vinegar)

2–4 tablespoons (15–30 grams) ice water, as needed

Additional gluten-free flour or sweet white rice flour for rolling
    out dough

CONTINUED ON PAGE 80

Kate's Gluten-Free Flour Mix

INGREDIENTS

· · · · ·

4½ cups (566 grams) tapioca starch

4¾ cups (623 grams) cornstarch

4⅓ cups (680 grams) sweet white rice flour

2 cups (340 grams) potato starch

TO MAKE 2½ CUPS (396 GRAMS), ENOUGH FOR ONE DOUBLE-CRUST PIE

¾ cup (95 grams) tapioca starch

¾ cup (98 grams) cornstarch

¾ cup (116 grams) sweet white rice flour

¼ cup (87 grams) potato starch

PROCEDURE

· · · · ·

1. Mix all ingredients together well in a big bowl.
2. Store in a glass jar or other storage container of your choice.

· **NOTE** · · · · · · · · · · · · · · · · · ·
Mochiko sweet mochi rice flour can be used in place of
sweet white rice flour.
· ·

PROCEDURE
· · · · ·

1. Place the flour mix, salt, sugar, butter, and leaf lard in the work bowl of a food processor and pulse to break up the pieces of fat incompletely.

2. Add the eggs, vinegar, and 2 tablespoons (30 grams) of ice water and pulse 5 to 10 times more. If the dough isn't coming together, add more water, 1 to 2 teaspoons at a time, and pulse again until the dough begins to come together without forming a complete ball. The dough will feel kind of squishy . . . sort of like a well-known "Dough Boy."

3. Remove the dough from the work bowl, place it on a sheet of plastic wrap, and divide the ball of dough in half to form two chubby discs roughly the size of hockey pucks.

4. Wrap each disc separately in plastic, and place them in the fridge to chill the fats for at least one hour.

ROLLING INSTRUCTIONS

. . . . .

1. Unwrap one disc of chilled dough and place it on a large sheet of plastic wrap that has been dusted with sweet white rice flour or Gluten-Free Flour Mix (page 79). Sprinkle another teaspoon on top of the dough and cover it with an additional large sheet of plastic wrap.

2. With a light touch, quickly roll out the dough to approximately 9 to 10 inches (23 to 25 centimeters) in diameter and ¼- to ½-inch thick (a bit less than 1 centimeter).

3. With plastic on BOTH sides, drape the dough over the rolling pin and carefully peel off the outer layer of plastic wrap. The inside plastic layer will be touching the pin.

4. Carefully place the dough-covered rolling pin in the middle of the pie pan.

5. Unfold the dough and keep the plastic wrap on.

6. Use your fingers to adjust and smooth the dough. There may be some overhang of dough on the sides of the pan.

7. With the plastic wrap still in place, place the dough-filled pie pan in the fridge or freezer for a few minutes to re-chill.

8. When chilled carefully, peel the plastic off using quick little tugs and fill the pie pan with already prepared filling.

9. Roll out the top dough as before and place it on top of the filling. Keeping the plastic in place, adjust the top as needed. Pinch off extra dough around the edge. With plastic wrap covering the edge, carefully crimp or finish as desired. Carefully remove the plastic wrap using quick little tugs.

10. To vent, cut one circle about 1½ inches (about 3.5 centimeters) in diameter and remove.

11. Chill until you're ready to bake.

Gluten-Free All-Butter Dough

This is the all-butter version of the gluten-free dough. Use a food processor to make it. Your hands will never touch the dough, not during the making nor the rolling—there will always be a layer of plastic wrap between you and the dough. I suggest you read through the directions for rolling out several times before doing it for the first time (see page 81).

FOR ONE DOUBLE-CRUST PIE OR TWO SINGLE-CRUST PIES

INGREDIENTS
· · · · ·

2½ cups (396 grams) Kate's Gluten-Free Flour Mix (page 79)

½ teaspoon (3 grams) salt

1 tablespoon (12 grams) granulated sugar (optional)

14 tablespoons (196 grams) salted or unsalted butter, cut into tablespoon-size pieces

2 large eggs, fork-beaten

1 tablespoon (15 grams) apple cider vinegar (Bragg's or another artisan apple cider vinegar)

2–4 tablespoons (30–60 grams) ice water, as needed

Additional gluten-free flour or sweet white rice flour for rolling out dough

PROCEDURE

· · · · ·

1. Place the flour mix, salt, sugar, and butter in the work bowl of a food processor and pulse to break up the pieces of fat incompletely.

2. Add the eggs, vinegar, and 2 tablespoons (30 grams) of ice water and pulse 5 to 10 times more. If it needs more water, add it now, 1 to 2 teaspoons at a time, and pulse again until the dough begins to come together without forming a complete ball. The dough will feel kind of squishy . . . sort of like a well-known "Dough Boy."

3. Remove the dough from the work bowl, place it on a sheet of plastic wrap, and divide the ball of dough in half to form two chubby discs roughly the size of hockey pucks.

4. Wrap each disc separately in plastic, and place them in the fridge to chill the fats back up for at least one hour.

5. See page 81 for rolling instructions.

Gluten-Free Butter and Shortening Dough

This is the butter and shortening version of the gluten-free dough. The technique for making and rolling this dough is very different from gluten-full dough. Use a food processor to make it. You will have a layer of plastic wrap between you and the dough at all times. I suggest that you read through the directions (see page 81) for rolling out several times before doing it for the first time. Omit the sugar if you are using this dough for a savory pie.

FOR ONE DOUBLE-CRUST PIE OR TWO SINGLE-CRUST PIES

INGREDIENTS
· · · · ·

2½ cups (396 grams) Kate's Gluten-Free Flour Mix (page 79)

½ teaspoon (3 grams) salt

1 tablespoon (12 grams) sugar (optional)

8 tablespoons (112 grams) salted or unsalted butter, cut into tablespoon-size pieces

8 tablespoons (112 grams) vegetable shortening, cut into tablespoon-size pieces

2 large eggs, fork-beaten

1 tablespoon (15 grams) apple cider vinegar (Bragg's or another artisan apple cider vinegar)

2–4 tablespoons (15–30 grams) ice water, as needed

Additional gluten-free flour or sweet white rice flour for rolling out dough

PROCEDURE

· · · · ·

1. Place the flour mix, salt, sugar, butter, and shortening in the work bowl of a food processor and pulse to break up the pieces of fat incompletely.

2. Add the eggs, vinegar, and 2 tablespoons (30 grams) of ice water and pulse 5 to 10 times more. If it needs more water, add it now, 1 to 2 teaspoons at a time, and pulse again until the dough begins to come together without forming a complete ball. The dough will feel kind of squishy . . . sort of like a well-known "Dough Boy."

3. Remove the dough from the work bowl, place it on a sheet of plastic wrap, and divide the ball of dough in half to form two chubby discs roughly the size of hockey pucks.

4. Wrap each disc separately in plastic, and place them in the fridge to chill the fats for at least one hour.

5. See page 81 for rolling instructions.

Gluten-Free Cheddar Cheese Dough

When baked, this dough will have a little freckling on top where the cheese bits make their presence known. As I am gluten-free, I use this dough to top off my savory pies.

FOR ONE DOUBLE-CRUST PIE OR TWO SINGLE-CRUST PIES

INGREDIENTS
· · · · ·

2½ cups (396 grams) Kate's Gluten-Free Flour Mix (page 79)

½ teaspoon (3 grams) salt

8 tablespoons (112 grams) salted or unsalted butter, cut into tablespoon-size pieces, or a combination of butter and leaf lard

¼ pound (115 grams) Kerrygold Dubliner Cheese or other sharp cheddar cheese, grated and chopped fine with a knife

2 large eggs, fork-beaten

1 tablespoon (15 grams) apple cider vinegar (Bragg's or another artisan apple cider vinegar)

2–4 tablespoons (15–30 grams) ice water, as needed

Additional flour or sweet white rice flour for rolling out dough

PROCEDURE

· · · · ·

1. Place the flour mix, salt, butter, and cheddar cheese in the work bowl of a food processor and pulse to break up the pieces of fat incompletely.

2. Add the eggs, vinegar, and 2 tablespoons (30 grams) of ice water and pulse 5 to 10 times more. If it needs more water, add it now, 1 to 2 teaspoons at a time, and pulse again until the dough begins to come together without forming a complete ball.

3. Remove the dough from the work bowl, place it on a sheet of plastic wrap, and divide the ball of dough in half to form two chubby discs roughly the size of hockey pucks.

4. Wrap each disc separately in plastic, and place them in the fridge to chill the fats for at least one hour.

5. See page 81 for rolling instructions.

Gluten-Free Vegan Pie Dough

During the teenage years, there always seems to be one house known as "The Food House," a place to fuel up and land a good meal. During my son Duncan's high school years, our house was that spot, and a steady stream of young men, with insatiable appetites, raided my icebox and pantry shelves regularly. If there was food on the table, they were sure to show up . . . all of them. Even though my food budget far outdistanced my mortgage payments, I never regretted this. I got to know my son's friends, as well as keep a bit of an eye on them. If you are in the teenage parenting years yourself, you might want to consider this tactic. I probably did not know the half of all their escapades and most likely wouldn't have wanted to either, but when they were under my roof I knew they were safe . . . and well fed.

Now that they're all grown up, it's a joy when they drop by to say hello and have a slice or two when in town. One holiday season, I was deep into the R&D for my gluten-free vegan dough and needed some willing tasters. Because so many of the crew had sampled pies I had baked over the years, when the call went out there was no trouble drafting those who were in town. I knew that they would give me their honest opinions.

Creating gluten-free vegan dough was quite a challenge. Dairy and egg were out, and as I don't use gums, I needed to find something that would hold the dough together without making it tough. My first attempts were less than stellar. Nainoa, always a willing tester, haltingly yet politely said, "This . . . is the best . . . gluten-free . . . vegan crust . . . I've ever had." The look on his face belied those words, so I asked, "Have you ever had a gluten-free vegan crust before, Nainoa?" His one-word reply was "No." All who tried that experiment agreed that the texture was more like a shingle than tender piecrust. The improvements in my next efforts weren't much better, but they were game to continue tasting, so I kept baking.

I tried ingredients and techniques I had read about to hold the dough together: applesauce, chia seed, flax seed both soaked and unsoaked, sometimes ground, and other times not. "Getting better, but still a ways to go," was always the verdict. The ground chia and flax seeds were definitely on the "keep" list. But when I added psyllium powder made from husks, I hit pay dirt. Gluten-free baker Jean Layton calls this mix "Pixie Dust," and I believe she is an absolute genius for figuring it out. I worked on adjusting the fats next and after more trial and more error found that my best results were achieved with a combination of a vegan "buttery stick" . . . and Crisco. Yes, the stuff in the blue can that I had eschewed for years had finally won that hard-earned place on my baking shelf. The combination of the two fats, plus Jean's "Pixie Dust," got me the coveted thumbs up from my testers.

This dough is a bit sandier then traditional pie dough, and like any gluten-free dough I have worked with it is more fragile. Please refer to the section on making and rolling gluten-free dough on page 72 and use the techniques detailed there for making, rolling, and finishing.

FOR ONE DOUBLE-CRUST PIE OR TWO SINGLE-CRUST PIES

INGREDIENTS
· · · · ·

2⅓ cups (370 grams) Kate's Gluten-Free Flour Mix (page 79)

⅓ cup (41 grams) sorghum flour

½ teaspoon (3 grams) salt

1 tablespoon (12 grams) sugar

2 teaspoons Jean Layton's Pixie Dust (recipe follows)

8 tablespoons (112 grams) vegan butter stick

8 tablespoons (112 grams) vegetable shortening

1 tablespoon (15 grams) apple cider vinegar (Bragg's or another artisan apple cider vinegar)

5–7 tablespoons (60–84 grams) ice water

Additional gluten-free flour or sweet white rice flour for rolling out dough

CONTINUED

PROCEDURE

· · · · ·

1. Mix the dry ingredients together and place them in a food processor.
2. Add all the fats, cut up into tablespoons-size pieces, and pulse 15 to 20 times.
3. Add the vinegar and pulse 5 times more.
4. Add 5 tablespoons (60 grams) of water and pulse 10 times.
5. The dough should feel very soft and somewhat sticky. Add more ice water if needed.
6. Scrape the dough out of the food processor and quickly pull it all together into a large ball about the size of a softball.
7. Divide the dough in half, wrap each half in plastic, and form each into a chubby disc about the size of a hockey puck.
8. Chill the dough for 2 hours.

ROLLING INSTRUCTIONS

· · · · ·

1. Unwrap one disc of chilled dough and place it on a large sheet of plastic wrap that has been dusted with sweet white rice flour or Gluten-Free Flour Mix (page 79). Sprinkle another teaspoon on top of the dough and cover it with an additional large sheet of plastic wrap.
2. With a light touch, quickly roll out the dough to approximately 9 to 10 inches (23 to 25 centimeters) in diameter and ¼ to ⅓ inch thick (a bit less than 1 centimeter).
3. With plastic on BOTH sides, drape the dough over the rolling pin and carefully peel off the outer layer of plastic wrap. The inside plastic layer will be touching the pin.
4. Carefully place the dough-covered rolling pin in the middle of the pie pan.
5. Unfold the dough and keep the plastic wrap on.
6. Use your fingers to adjust and smooth the dough. There may be some overhang of dough on the sides of the pan.

7. With the plastic wrap still in place, place the dough-filled pie pan in the fridge or freezer for a few minutes to re-chill.

8. When chilled, carefully peel the plastic off using quick little tugs and fill the pie pan with already prepared filling.

9. Roll out the top dough as before and place it on top of the filling. Keeping the plastic in place, adjust the top as needed. Pinch off any extra dough around the edge. With plastic wrap covering the edge, carefully crimp or finish as desired. Carefully remove the plastic wrap using quick little tugs.

10. To vent, cut one circle about 1½ inches (about 3.5 centimeters) in diameter and remove.

11. Chill, and before baking brush with an almond, hemp, or soy milk wash.

Jean Layton's Pixie Dust

INGREDIENTS

· · · · ·

3 parts golden flax seeds

2 parts chia seeds, either black or white

1 part psyllium powder

INSTRUCTIONS

· · · · ·

1. Grind the ingredients in the coffee grinder until the mixture is floury.

2. Store the mixture in the freezer until needed.

Gluten-Free Nutty No-Bake Crust

This is another very easy crust, since it requires absolutely no baking. You can use up to half of each nut flour, also known as meal, or all almond flour. Pair this crust with a Mocha Cream Pie (see page 286).

FOR ONE SINGLE-CRUST 9-INCH SHALLOW PIE

INGREDIENTS
· · · · ·

1 cup (112 grams) almond meal (also known as almond flour)

1 cup (89 grams) hazelnut meal (also known as hazelnut flour)

2 tablespoons (24 grams) sugar

¼ teaspoon salt (a pinch)

5 tablespoons (70 grams) butter (salted or unsalted), melted

PROCEDURE
· · · · ·

1. Place all the dry ingredients in a bowl and add the melted butter.
2. Mix together with clean hands or a fork until all the ingredients are well incorporated.
3. Pour the mixture into a pie pan, spread out evenly, and press firmly into place.
4. Chill for 2 hours before using.

Cookie Crumb Crust

This crust has only two ingredients and is a very quick and easy alternative to a pastry dough. I make it with chocolate cookies for my mom's Grasshopper Pie (see page 275). Ginger snaps are delicious with a Berry Tart with Vanilla Cream (see page 279), as are lemon crisps. Gluten-free cookies work as well.

FOR ONE SINGLE-CRUST 9-INCH SHALLOW PIE

INGREDIENTS
· · · · ·

12 cookies (7 ounces or 198 grams), enough to make 1½ cups cookie crumbs

4 tablespoons (56 grams) salted butter, melted

INSTRUCTIONS
· · · · ·

1. Place the whole cookies of your choice in a food processor with a metal blade and process the cookies until they are the size of coarse salt. You can also place them in a zipped plastic freezer bag and roll with a pin until they are crumbs.

2. Pour the crumbs into a bowl, add melted butter, and distribute well with clean hands or a fork.

3. Spread the mixture evenly into your pie plate or pan.

4. Place a sheet of parchment paper over the butter crumb mixture, and place a slightly smaller pie pan or a glass on top of the paper. Gently press or tap down, and slide it around all the surfaces, so that the bottom and sides will be the same thickness.

5. Place the crust into the refrigerator to chill while you make the filling.

Crumble Topping

Crumble toppings are a nice variation to top off a fruit pie. They can brown too much before the filling is done, so wait for the last twenty minutes of the bake to sprinkle this oat crumble evenly over the filling. If I have a disc of pie dough and pre-made oat crumble topping already in the freezer, making a pie is a snap. Use gluten-free flour and oats for those who require them.

TOPPING FOR ONE 9-INCH PIE

INGREDIENTS
· · · · ·

½ cup (110 grams) brown sugar, packed

¼ teaspoon salt (a pinch)

½ cup (73 grams) flour

1½ cups (144 grams) whole oats

8 tablespoons (112 grams) unsalted butter

½ cup (60 grams) pecans, chopped (optional)

PROCEDURE
· · · · ·

1. Put the brown sugar, salt, flour, and oats in the bowl of a food processor and pulse a few times to mix.
2. Cut the chilled butter into 8 large pieces and place them in the food processor bowl. Pulse the food processor about 20 times to cut the butter into the dry ingredients. It should look crumbly. Pulse more if needed.
3. Add the optional chopped nuts to the crumble mixture and pulse a few more times.
4. Pour the mixture into a bowl or plastic bag and chill in the freezer for at least 15 minutes while you make the filling.

Blind Baking, or Pre-Baking a Crust

You'll need to keep your eyes open when you blind bake a crust. Simply put, you will pre-bake a pie shell minus the filling. When the shell cools, it can be used for a pie that does not need to go into the oven for a full bake, like lemon meringue. You'll use pie weights, which can be beans, rice, ceramic, or metal, placed on top of parchment paper or aluminum foil, to help keep the dough from rising up with bubbles. The first time I blind baked, I placed beans directly onto the unbaked dough. When I pulled the pan from the oven and had to pick the hot beans off the dough, I quickly realized it is necessary to have something between the dough and the weights. I'm also including a variation that uses finely crushed crumbs, which keeps the crust very crispy. Shirley Corriher suggests using the rolled-in-crumbs technique for custard pies in her book *Bakewise*.

PROCEDURE

. . . . .

1. Roll out dough 2 inches (5 centimeters) larger than the size of your pie pan. Gently place it in a chilled pie pan. Flute or crimp the edges. The dough may shrink some in the bake so be sure it extends all the way to the edge of the pie pan.

2. Dock the dough by lightly piercing the bottom and sides with a fork.

3. Cover with plastic and place in freezer until frozen (at least 30 minutes). The freezing helps with the shrinkage of the crust during the bake, although there may still be some.

4. Remove plastic wrap, and cover dough with a sheet of parchment paper (or aluminum foil) that is cut about 2 inches (5 centimeters) larger than your pie pan. Be sure to cut the paper large, as you need enough above the rim of the pie pan so you can lift the hot pie weights out. You don't want to spill the beans into the pie crust or onto the floor, which I learned the hard way.

5. Fill with pie weights of choice.

6. In an oven preheated to 375°F (190°C), bake the pie shell for 20 to 25 minutes.

7. Remove from oven, and carefully take out the parchment paper and weights. If a bit of the dough has stuck onto the backside of the parchment because of the weight of the beans, no one will ever know if you scrape it off and gently pat it back onto the spot in the crust where it came from. Keep the pie weights for your next blind baking session.

8. Put the pie back in the oven and bake for another 10 minutes at 325°F (162°C) to dry out the crust more and give it a golden color.

9. Remove from oven and cool completely before using.

VARIATION

· · · · ·

BLIND BAKED ON COOKIE CRUMBS Crush about 6 cookies inside a plastic freezer bag with a rolling pin to break them up (¼ cup or 2 ounces crumbs), then put them through a mesh sieve to sift more finely. Spread the crumbs out on your rolling surface, place the dough on top of them, and roll so that the crumbs are on the bottom of the dough only. Place the dough in the pan, crumb-side down. Follow from step 3 in the blind baking recipe but watch the timing—this crust will cook faster so bake for 15 minutes at 375°F (190°C), remove the weights, then bake at 325°F (162°C) for 5 minutes or until edges are brown.

CHAPTER TWO

Fruit, Sweetener, Seasoning, and Thickener

How to Fill and Finish Your Pie

I did not like fruit or vegetables when I was a little

girl at all. Maybe that had something to do with growing up in the 1950s, when most of what was on my dinner plate came from a can or out of the freezer, the then-modern and convenient way for women to feed their families. At school it was nearly the same. Every day I walked down the hall to the big cafeteria where "the lunch ladies" fed us. We ate off metal trays with three sections: the biggest one for sloppy Joes, grilled cheese sandwiches, or pasta with red sauce; the two smaller sections had canned peas or beans and the fruit of the day, which many times was sicky sweet canned pear halves, my least favorite of all fruits. I could never bring myself to eat more than a bite and the rest was still on my tray when I left the cafeteria. One day the lead lunchroom lady came over to my seat, bent over, and hissed in my ear, "You best not leave those pears again." I was absolutely mortified and, to this day, I remember my cheeks getting hot.

At home that night I pleaded with my mom to "let me bring my own lunch to school like all my other friends, puleeze," and wonder of wonders, she agreed. We went shopping for a lunch box that Saturday, and I picked out a red plaid metal one with a thermos that fit neatly inside. I was so proud to bring it to school the following Monday. My very first lunch from home was a PB&J made with squishy white balloon bread wrapped in brown wax paper, two yummy chocolate sandwich cookies, and a little paper Dixie cup container with a tiny wooden spoon on top. "Ooooo," I thought, "a surprise." I pulled up the little tab on the white paper top, only to find canned pears staring me straight in the face—the same darn ones from the lunchroom. Was there no mercy? What would happen to all the starving children in China if I tossed the pears, applesauce, canned peaches, and fruit cocktail, which followed on a regular rotation, into the trash? Would I have to confess this to Father Whalen before receiving communion?

I hated my lunch and my chubby body, too. My mom and grandmother wanted me to have the same trim ankles and shapely calves that they did, but since I am adopted, this is apparently not in my genetic makeup. Diet pills were all the rage, and by the age of ten, Mom had gotten our family doctor to prescribe them for me. Along with fresh squeezed orange juice, I took a little white pill daily. There were weekly weigh-in visits and a nurse who called out my weight loud enough so that everyone in the waiting room could hear. Although it was mortifying, I learned it was easiest to just keep quiet, and get it over with as soon as possible. When I graduated from sixth grade, Mom signed me up for a reducing salon. I was the youngest of a coterie of middle-age housewives. Before a jiggling conveyor belt was placed around my hips and thighs to "break down the fat," a report of every bite I had eaten had to be given to the salon counselors, who also weighed and measured me. I remember my grandmother, Geeg, saying once, "Won't it be nice when you go to your new school. No one will ever know you were fat." I'm sure it was meant as an "atta girl," but it hurt deeply to hear.

Even after I lost weight, the humiliation didn't stop when I went to my new school. On Friday nights, we were sent to ballroom dance classes taught by Miss O'Brien. Being the last one asked to dance probably had more to do with my dress, a sensible long-sleeve dark gray wool number trimmed with an antiquated white lace collar, during a time when all the popular girls had long blond hair, and wore miniskirts à la Twiggy. When I look back at pictures taken of me during my youth, I see that I wasn't ever fat. But no matter what I did, or how skinny I got, I was never going to have the body that Mom and Geeg desired for me. In some ways, I feel that the experience has given me a certain empathy with pie makers, who feel that their pies will never live up to the perfect ones seen on the covers and in the centerfolds of glossy food magazines.

By late high school, the "back to the land" movement had entered our town full tilt. It was a relief to be able to wear long-skirted granny dresses that covered my legs, and have my wavy dark brown hair fall loose down my back. Mom was petrified that I would run away and join the commune in the mountains outside of town, but the closest I ever got to that was shopping at the commune's natural foods store and looking at the photos of handsome hippie men tilling the land with horse-drawn plows that were displayed on the store's walls. My girlfriends and I fantasized about homesteading with them. I bought an organic apple at the store that tasted nothing like the sugary applesauce of my early school lunches. It was tart and sweet, juicy and crisp, and sent a shocking current of flavor through me that reset my entire system. I was hooked and, for the first time in my life, found myself enjoying fruit. Next came strawberries, cherries, and, finally, the pears that only a decade before I would have left uneaten. Add in whole grains, yogurt, and local organic veggies, and my world and identity were expanding in a crunchy, "granola" sort of way.

Thirty-five years later I had become a regular at my farmers' market, and enjoyed being known as that pie-making fruit buyer. During the fall apple and pear harvest season, Saturday market day was the highlight of my week. In addition to smiles and hugs, my favorite growers gave me samples of flavorful apples and pears, and we chatted while I considered what each would contribute to a pie. In the end, I would go home with some of every variety they brought to market.

The Fruit Year

Some count the year by months; I mark its passage by the seasons. I used to joke that my homeschooled boy may not have known the days of the week as soon as some of his age-mates did, but he absolutely knew the seasons of the year and what happened in them. Peas are planted in early spring, and garlic in the fall. To make spaghetti sauce to can or freeze for use in the winter, tomatoes and basil need the warm sunny days of summer. Strawberry plants are divided and replanted in the fall, so we can add berries to a rhubarb pie and make fresh shortcake in June and July . . . and always we save seeds so we can grow more the following year.

If pricey out-of-season produce from another continent showed up in our farm store during the winter, like grapes, we passed them by and watched and waited for our local varieties to ripen months later. Then we added bunches of sweet carrots grown on Nash's farm to our basket of winter root vegetables. When the local grape season finally rolled around, we bought as many as we could and enjoyed every sweet bite.

Starting with the apple harvest in the fall, my fruit year for pie goes something like this:

FALL	WINTER	SPRING	SUMMER
Apples	Lemons	Rhubarb	Apricots
Grapes	Oranges	Strawberries	Peaches
Pears		Sour Cherries	Nectarines
Quince			Raspberries
Pumpkins			Marionberries
Squash			Gooseberries
Nuts			Currants
			Salmonberries
			Blueberries
			Blackberries

Since the weather plays an important part when buying locally and seasonally, some years I don't get everything I'm hoping to put in a pie. I may miss out on special varieties of apples if a farmer has a bad year, like in 2013 when hailstorms badly battered the crops of Cox Orange, Newtown Pippin, Golden Russet, and many others that I love to add to my apple pies; or the lack of huckleberries in Washington State due to drought and the fires of 2015. Like best friends from out of town who come to visit annually, the seasonal ripening of local fruits is a much-anticipated rhythm of my year.

Photo credit: Leigh Olson

My cottage didn't start out to be Pie Cottage. I

didn't wake up one morning and say, "Gosh, I think I'll buy a little house, decorate it with pie-related memorabilia, and call it Pie Cottage." In fact, like so much of my life, it just happened. If I were to give it a starting place, I believe it might be the day my first grade teacher, Mrs. Anderson, passed out crayons and pieces of drawing paper. The assignment was to draw and color the house where each of us lived. I drew a house with a peaked roof, sash windows on each side of the front door, and even though the house I lived in was white, I colored it light blue with a pink door, resulting in the school principal—who my grandmother knew well—to call my mom to find out if everything was okay at home. I can't imagine a principal doing that today. Can you? I finished it off with some big puffy clouds and rays shooting out from a round yellow sun. I had drawn Pie Cottage, the home that I would create and put my heart and soul into some forty years later.

Duncan was not thrilled when we first saw the house. It was small, and for the first time in his life there would be neighbors close by. We had previously lived in a remote mountain cabin with Duncan's dad; after his father unexpectedly left us, I was ready to sell and begin again with a more manageable house in town.

When the day came that I had saved enough for a down payment, my best friend, Nancy, called to let me know that just around the corner from her was a cute cottage with a "for sale" sign in the front yard. I called my real estate agent and an hour later we walked through the door. Nancy was right—it was very cute. There was a fenced backyard, bearing apple trees, a stunning view of the snow-capped Olympic Mountains, peek-a-boo view of the water, old growth fir floors, a woodstove, a peaked roof, and two sash windows on either side of the front

door, just like the little blue house I had drawn in first grade. I placed an offer on the spot, signed the final papers a month later, and moved in with our dog and cat, two grand pianos, crates of music, and my cookbooks. Buying it continues to be one of the best decisions I have ever made.

As I started down the path of pie making, I scoured estate sales for pie-related treasures. Pie pans, cookbooks, baskets, and servers, all could count on finding a home with me. Friends who knew of my passion began stopping by with fruit crate labels, antique rolling pins, and art prints of pies and fruit that I framed and put up on my walls. Folks who had taken my pie workshops sent me surprises of pie birds, hand-pie cutters, kitchen towels, aprons, and potholders with pie sayings on them. My collection of cookbooks spilled out onto every flat surface and available shelf, as I chanced upon well-used and sometimes collectible editions, and I still enjoy adding the newest titles to my ever-growing pie library. My favorite piece of all time though is the stained glass of a just baked pie cooling in a window that Duncan made for me. Prominently displayed in the front window of my cottage, it has become the logo for Art of the Pie. One day I referred to my periwinkle blue and teal–trimmed house with raspberry doors as Pie Cottage. I looked around at what I had created over fifteen years and instead of sounding cloyingly sweet, it seemed to capture the heart of my home.

My Pie Cottage garden is a reminder of an exceptionally sweet season of my life, when my days were centered on growing a family and feeding us from a very large organic garden. Although smaller in square footage, my city garden still seems quite large. For example, I think of the unattended fruit trees in my neighborhood as being part of it. On my daily walks with Gretapie, my German shepherd companion, I scope out the blossom time of sour cherries, pears, and nearby apple trees. I know where to find the sweetest blackberries within ten blocks, and though I won't tell you exactly where they are, if you follow me out the back door on a late summer's evening you'll find me in the briar picking them one by one into a little blue bucket. When it is filled it to the top, I have enough berries for a pie, plus a few

more for snacking and putting on top of my morning oats.

Fifteen miles east of me, down a dirt lane, is my friend Melissa's five acres. Melissa grows apples, pears, sour pie cherries, raspberries, blackberries, blueberries, grapes, herbs, flowers, chickens, and lambs. When I need fruit for a workshop, she is my first stop. The rhubarb I harvest from her plants is the biggest and best I have found anywhere. She lives a sweet and simple life as a gardener and weaver, and is one of the happiest and kindest people I know.

Farmers Nash and Patty Huber, who have been friends for over thirty years, farm in the fertile soil of the Dungeness River Delta. In my savory pies, I bake up Nash's greens and root vegetables, and look forward to buying from his crew on Saturday mornings at my local farmers' market. Nash's carrots are so sweet that when Duncan turned twelve he and his friends ate up the carrots and left the cake. Every autumn I offer a pie-making demonstration at his farm store as a thank you for being part of my garden, and I always bring three or four big slab pies to the legendary potluck and barn dances held in the packing shed at his farm. Gathering with others who live in the shadow of the Olympic Mountains reminds me that life is made richer and sweeter when you're part of a larger community.

Use All the Senses When Making Pie

SIGHT: Use your eyes when you fill the pie pan with fruit. Too much? Too little? Just right? When the pie is about halfway through its bake time, turn on the oven light and open the door to take a quick peek. What did you see? Is the top of the pie already a golden brown color, or are the edges browning too fast? If too fast, cover it loosely with a foil tent with a vent torn in the middle. Place the shiny side down, since that side deflects heat, and keep on baking. Before it's due to come out of the oven, check once more to see if the fruit filling is happily and steadily bubbling through the vents, a sure sign that it is done.

SOUND: After you take the pie out of the oven, pull your hair back, and get your ear really close to the top so you can hear its sizzle-whump. The sizzle is all the fat in the crust. The whump is the fruit filling bubbling up and hitting the inside of the upper crust, which some call the heartbeat of the pie. These are two of my favorite sounds in pie making, plus the sound a crisp and flaky crust makes when being cut.

SMELL: When the pie is in the oven and the house smells like a bakery, it's about 80 percent done.

TASTE: The filling needs to taste good to you. After adding and mixing together fruit, sweetener, seasoning, and thickener, take a taste, and stop if you like it. If not, adjust the sweetener or seasoning to what you do like, and not what any recipe tells you. You are the boss.

TOUCH: Make sure your pie has cooled to the touch before you cut into it, so the fruit filling has a chance to properly set up and is cool enough to eat. In 1862, Henry Ward Beecher wrote in his essay "Apple Pie" that "It reaches its highest state about one hour after it comes from the oven, and just before its natural heat has quite departed."

ENJOYMENT: The most important sense of all. Enjoy every step of the making, baking, and sharing with family and friends, as well as the stories, history, and the anticipation of the next pie to come. After every slice has been eaten and it appears there is nothing in your pie pan but a few crumbs and traces of fruit filling, check again. It is likely that it has been refilled with a whole lot of love.

TRUST YOURSELF: If you are doing something else while your pie is baking and you have a sense that you should check on the pie, stop and go see to it. You may catch the pie just before the top is about to burn or bubble over with filling onto the oven floor.

Best Fruit Filling
(The Long Wordy Version)

Fruit, sweetener, seasoning, and thickener: just as there are four ingredients that go into pie dough, there are four categories of ingredients that go into a seasonal fruit pie filling, with plenty of room for experimentation and variation. Use this recipe as a starting place and then branch out to add your own spin, but these basic four categories will always remain the same.

FRUIT: We need fruit, but not just any fruit. For a top-notch pie we need what I call "pie-worthy" fruit. This is fruit with flavor that dances on your tongue and sends little currents and shivers of sweet and tart right through you. "Pie-worthy" fruit makes you want to take a second and even a third bite before it goes into the filling. If you have ever tasted a sweet, juicy peach and exclaimed, or even moaned, "Oh. My. God!" then you know what "pie-worthy" fruit is all about. Once you experience flavor like this, it's hard, if not impossible, to return to fruit with lackluster flavor. No matter how much sweetener or seasoning you add, all you will taste is sugar and spice. There is absolutely nothing that can make up for missing fruit flavor. Be sure to shop local as often as you can and establish sustainable relationships within your own community. Ask your greengrocer and the vendors at farmers' markets what is ripe and ready that day, then request a taste. Produce managers and farmers should be proud of what they offer you in exchange for your hard-earned dollars. If they say "no" to giving a sample, then you might be shopping at the wrong market. Most are delighted to share tips on what is sweet and seasonal, as well as what will be coming along next week, too. They will know you for a savvy buyer and one who has good taste when you ask about the fruit.

· · · · · · A QUICK WORD ABOUT USING FROZEN FRUIT · · · · · ·

Frozen fruit may be used in fruit pie. Do not thaw frozen
fruit but use it as if it were fresh when making the filling.
Thawed fruit will make a filling that is very runny.

· ·

HOW MUCH FRUIT IN A FILLING: I generally size my recipes for 9-inch deep-dish pie pans, but this is just a starting point. It is fine if the pie pan you choose to use is larger or smaller than mine. Just fill the pan with enough seasonal "pie-worthy" fruit to reach the rim. For exceptionally juicy fruits like rhubarb, cherries, berries, and peaches, do not overfill the pie pan. Let me repeat that, in case you did not hear me: **do not overfill the pie pan!** One-half inch below the rim of the pie pan is the place to stop. You may be tempted to overfill, thinking more is better, but that pie will bubble over and much of your delicious filling will be smoking on your oven floor. Save the mounding up for big mile-high apple or pear pies; these are the two fruits you can pile as high as you like. Be sure to buy extra for tasting and snacking.

· · · · · · · · · · FREEZING FRUIT FOR LATER · · · · · · · · · ·

During the fruit-bearing months of spring, summer, and fall, when gardens and orchards give us a choice of many sweet offerings, I freeze as much of the harvest as I can in plastic bags placed in a chest freezer that sits on my back porch. There is an undeniable feeling of wealth and prosperity when lifting the freezer lid to see all the strawberries, blackberries, raspberries, and my favorite sour pie cherries from neighborhood trees, farmers' markets, and my own garden tucked inside.

Choose ripe fruit with peak flavor, local and organic whenever possible. Slice or chop the fruit to a size you will use in your pie filling—an easy way to think of this might be to cut pieces to a size you can comfortably put into your mouth. Cut out any noticeably spoiled sections. Spread the pieces out on parchment paper–covered trays, then place them in the freezer until they're frozen solid. I once placed my entire harvest of homegrown Shuksan strawberries directly into a freezer bag before freezing them on trays. When I pulled a bag out to use in a strawberry rhubarb pie, I had a big lump of frozen strawberries that required an ice pick to break apart.

Mark your freezer bags with the name of the fruit inside and the date of its harvest. Pour in the frozen fruit, seal the bag up well, and place the bag back in the freezer, taking care that the fruit does not defrost in the process.

If you want to make it even easier to use your summer fruit during winter, you can make and freeze fillings pre-formed into discs, which can later be placed directly into a waiting, unbaked pie shell.

- With sturdy plastic wrap, smoothly line a pie pan that is slightly smaller than the one you ultimately plan to bake the pie in. Pour the fruit filling into the plastic–lined pan.
- Place the filled pan in the freezer on a flat surface and remove when frozen. Lift the disc of fruit filling from the pan. Double-wrap, date it, and place it back into the freezer. (It will last up to six months.)
- When it is time to bake, pull the disc out of the freezer, unwrap and place it, unthawed, into an unbaked pie shell in a pie pan that is slightly larger than the frozen disc.
- Be sure to add 15 to 20 minutes extra baking time.

· ·

SWEETENER: I use granulated cane sugar. It's readily available and is what my grandmother used. There's nothing exotic about it. If you like, bury a vanilla bean in the bag for a couple of weeks, which will give a lovely scent and flavor perfect for pear pie. Dark or light brown, date or turbinado—you can use any sugar that strikes your fancy, and each will have a flavor that comes through in the filling. Blond-colored turbinado sugar has a mild brown sugar flavor; dark brown sugar has a stronger molasses flavor; and date sugar does taste like dates. I don't work with sugarless sweeteners, but I did taste a very good pie at a potluck that had been made with a sugar substitute. The pie maker told me that she followed her regular recipe, using sugar substitute, and it baked up fine.

Taste the fruit and then add sugar according to what it needs and not what the recipe tells you to do, even mine. Err on the less sweet side. It's easy to add sugar but much harder to take it away.

My general rule of thumb for sugaring a few popular fruit pies made in a 9-inch deep-dish pie pan is approximately:

- ½ cup (100 grams) for apples
- ¾ cup (75 grams) for blackberries, blueberries, raspberries, and stone fruits like peaches, plums, and apricots
- 1 cup (200 grams) for rhubarb
- 1¼ cups (225 grams) for sour cherry

If you are using a smaller pie pan than mine, then adjust down by adding less sugar, and if you are using a larger pie pan, add a bit more. Let your own taste be your guide. Swapping out honey for sugar is not something I do, but if you do, you'll need to add a bit more thickener.

SEASONING: There is no limit when it comes to seasoning, so let your imagination and taste be the guide. Sometimes all that is needed is a pinch of salt, squeeze of lemon, and grating of nutmeg. Apple pie is delicious with cinnamon, allspice, nutmeg, a squeeze of lemon or tablespoon of an artisan apple cider vinegar, and even a splash of applejack or Calvados. Whatever you choose to season your filling with, taste as you go so your "pie-worthy" fruit is always the star.

· · · · · · · · · · HOW FRESH ARE YOUR SPICES? · · · · · · · · · ·

- Spices lose potency and flavor as they age.
- The rule of thumb is that ground spices will last 6 months to 1 year, and whole spices up to 18 months.
- Store spices correctly: no extreme temperatures, either hot or cold, and in a dark cupboard away from light sources or in dark glass airtight jars.
- Only buy what you think you'll use in a 6-month to 1-year period. You can always buy more.
- Purchase from a reputable spice store that has a good turnover of inventory, or online (see Sources, page 338).

· ·

THICKENER: I use three main thickeners, individually and in tandem.

FLOUR: Unbleached all-purpose flour is a staple in my baking kitchen and an old standby for use as a thickener. Its thickening power is about half that of either cornstarch or tapioca. Flour gives a slight opacity to a filling. I use it to thicken the fillings in pear and apple pies.

TAPIOCA: Tapioca comes from the cassava root, and we use two main forms for pies: quick-cooking and starch, also known as tapioca flour. Tapioca gives fruit pies a clear glossy filling with no starchy flavor. Like cornstarch, tapioca has twice the thickening power of flour. At the end of a bake, make sure you see steady bubbling of the filling that can be glimpsed through the vents or latticework. That way you'll know that the tapioca has reached a high enough temperature to do its work. If tapioca doesn't reach a high enough temperature, you may find yourself with a layer of tapioca sludge, topped by fruit soup when you cut into that first slice. Quick-cooking tapioca is granular in form, and will soften but not dissolve completely in your fruit fillings, especially if steady bubbling is not seen at the end of a bake.

CORNSTARCH: I use cornstarch for fillings that are cooked on a stovetop like lemon meringue and flavored cream pies. Cornstarch has a noticeable flavor if not cooked completely, so be sure to cook it long enough for the filling to get good and thick, but not so long that you scorch the bottom of the pan. If too much cornstarch is used the filling will be gloppy. Cornstarch has twice the thickening power of flour. It does not thicken well when acidic liquids, like lemon juice, are added during the cooking. So, add your acidic liquids after the cornstarch has already thickened.

MIXING THICKENERS: There are many variables to consider in the moisture content of individual fruits, including seasonal weather patterns or a farm's microclimate. For example, when purchasing the first pick of rhubarb after a particularly wet spring, the farmer alerted me to the need for extra thickener. I find mixing two thickeners together can really help a filling from being too soupy, especially with rhubarb and berries. Adding a tablespoon or two of flour to the tapioca recommended in a recipe, or up to a tablespoon of tapioca to flour, will give your pie the perfect amount of ooze.

In a 9-inch deep-dish pie pan I use:

- ½ cup (73 grams) flour for apple or pear fillings
- 2–3 tablespoons (24–36 grams) tapioca for berries, sometimes followed by 1 tablespoon flour
- ⅓ cup (60 grams) quick-cooking tapioca for tart sour pie cherries, juicy peaches, and a deep-dish rhubarb pie

Remember to adjust a bit more or less, depending on the size of your pie pan.

PUTTING IT ALL TOGETHER: Once you have fruit, sweetener, seasoning, and thickener in the bowl, give it a stir with a spoon or a toss with your hands, and then take a taste. If it makes you want to take a second bite, you are there. If not, adjust with more sweetener, spices, or a liqueur to taste. When you can't stop yourself from taking more bites, it is ready to use. Set it aside to let the flavors "meet and greet," as author Elizabeth Berg says in her book, *The Day I Ate Whatever I Wanted*, and move on to rolling out the dough.

FINISHING IT ALL UP: Now roll out the dough and place it in your pie pan of choice. Turn in the filling with a spatula, spoon, or your hands. Top it with a full or lattice crust, place it in the fridge while you preheat the oven to 425°F (220°C), and clean up your counter. Just before you bake the pie, paint it lightly with an egg white wash, egg yolk wash for gluten-free doughs, or whatever wash the recipe calls for. I use a silicon brush for this but a paper towel or even your fingers will work in a pinch. Bake your pie for twenty minutes at 425°F (220°C) until you see a bit of golden browning on top, then turn the oven down to 375°F (190°C) and continue to bake for thirty to forty minutes more as needed. When there are ten to fifteen minutes left in the bake time, open the oven, pull out the rack with the pie on it, and quickly sprinkle the top of the pie evenly with a teaspoon or two (4-8 grams) of sugar. A teaspoon size mesh tea strainer works great for even sprinkling. Push the rack back in and continue to bake the pie. When the fruit filling is sending some bubbles up through the vents or lattice, and the top is a beautiful golden brown, take the pie out of the oven with potholders and set it on a cooling rack or windowsill to cool. The filling will continue to set up while cooling. Serve with a smile.

P.S. If you forget to sprinkle with sugar during the last fifteen minutes of the bake, sprinkle the sugar evenly over the top as soon as it comes out of the oven.

· · · · · · · · · · · · · · · · PIE CHILLING · · · · · · · · · · · · · · · ·

Ideally, you want to place a crust that is chilled—not warm—into your oven (remember Rule #1). If you can, especially on a hot day or if your hands or kitchen environment have made the fats in the dough melty, give the pie one last chill in the fridge for 20 minutes or so while the oven preheats.

Another trick is to chill the unbaked and unfilled pie shell. Just cover the unfilled crust with a layer of plastic wrap and keep it in the fridge while you make the filling. Then fill the unbaked shell and place it back in the fridge while you roll out your top dough.

You may not have time to do this, and it's not always necessary. (At my Pie Camps, we don't have room for six pies to cool in the fridge, so those go straight into the oven. They turn out just fine.) Many of my recipes begin with preheating the oven, which moves things along so you can eat your pie sooner.

In either case, when I remember, I set a baking sheet in the oven during the preheat and place the pie directly on it so that the bottom crust can get a good blast of direct heat when it begins its bake. This can help with the dreaded soggy bottom.

· ·

The Best Fruit Pie
(The Short Tidy Version)

For those who like a recipe written up all neat and tidy, here you go. You can use pretty much any fruit, fresh or frozen. If using frozen, you won't need to defrost it at all. Taste for sweetness and adjust the sugar accordingly. Feel free to try other seasonings as you like, because this is your pie.

THIS FRUIT FILLING IS FOR ONE 9-INCH DEEP-DISH PIE, BUT
ADJUST THE AMOUNTS UP OR DOWN FOR THE SIZE OF PAN YOU ARE USING

INGREDIENTS
. . . . .

6 cups, or about 1½– 2 pounds (680–900 grams) fruit, fresh or frozen; adjust for the size of the pan

½–1 cup (100–200 grams) granulated sugar, depending on the sweetness of the fruit

Small pinch of ground nutmeg

⅓ teaspoon (2 grams) salt

Small squeeze of lemon

¼ cup (36 grams) all-purpose unbleached flour (use dip and sweep method on page 36)

1–2 tablespoons (12–24 grams) quick-cooking tapioca, if your fruit is especially juicy

1 recipe double-crust pie dough

½ tablespoon (7 grams) butter

1–2 teaspoons (4–8 grams) sugar, for sprinkling on top of pie

EGG WASH

1 egg white (or yolk, for gluten-free crusts) plus 1 tablespoon (15 grams) water, fork beaten

PROCEDURE

· · · · ·

1. Preheat the oven to 425°F (220°C).

2. Put the fruit, sugar, nutmeg, salt, lemon, flour, and tapioca (optional) in a big bowl and mix lightly until the fruit is well coated.

3. Adjust the sweetener and seasonings to your taste.

4. Roll out your dough and place it in a chilled pie pan.

5. Pour the filling into the pan and dot with little pieces of butter.

6. Roll out the remaining dough, lay it over the fruit, and cut 5 to 6 vents on top; or cut strips and make a lattice top. Trim excess dough from the edges and crimp (see Vents, Appliqués, Crimps, Flutes, Lattice, pages 51–56).

7. Lightly brush some of the egg wash over the entire pie, including the edges.

8. Bake for 15 minutes at 425°F (220°C).

9. Reduce the heat to 375°F (190°C) and bake for 25 minutes. Open the oven and quickly sprinkle the top of pie with sugar. Close the oven and continue baking for another 10 to 15 minutes, or until you see the filling steadily bubbling.

10. Remove the pie from the oven. Let it cool completely so the filling can set up before serving.

· NOTE · · · · · · · · · · · · · · · · · · ·

This recipe uses the preheat first, no time to chill the pie method (see page 117), but use what works best for you depending on time and temperature.

· ·

My first baking "lessons" began before I was five

years old. With no written recipes, our neighbor, Sadie, showed me that the craft of baking is more than words on a printed page. We started with cookies. The ingredients and amounts differed slightly each time, but the results were always delicious.

Since I wasn't yet tall enough to work at her kitchen counter, she pulled up a sturdy chair from the dining room for me to stand on. For our measuring equipment, we used a coffee cup from the cupboard above and a silver teaspoon from the drawer below. She showed me how to fork-beat eggs in a cereal bowl until they were frothy and light, to cream butter and sugar using a hand-cranked beater, and to sweep extra flour off the top of the coffee cup with a knife edge to make it even. To measure salt, Sadie poured it directly into my hand from the round blue box with the picture of the little girl holding an umbrella. Sadie said she was pretty . . . like me. The crank handle of her silver-gray sifter had a worn red wooden knob on its end and I loved to turn it until the flour had sifted all the way through to form the shape of a perfect snow covered mountain. We mixed dry and wet ingredients in a crockery bowl using a big wooden spoon, and I got to take one taste of the batter with my finger (I always made sure it was a big one). When it was time to bake, Sadie taught me that using my eyes and nose were just as important as any kitchen timer, and to trust myself to know when the cookies were done. I loved seeing them come out all golden with slightly browned edges. After they had cooled enough, I sampled one or two at the big table, and washed them down with a cup of her strong Irish tea in the pretty pink flowered cup and saucer she saved especially for me.

Slab Fruit Pie

A slab pie with seasonal fruit is perfect for potlucks or big family gatherings. Make a double recipe of both the dough and the filling of your choice, and you'll be the favorite at the party for bringing a pie that serves twelve to twenty-four. Use a rimmed sheet pan, which is not quite as deep as a regular pie pan.

MAKES 1 (12-INCH × 17-INCH) PIE

INGREDIENTS
· · · · ·

1 recipe double-crust pie dough

2 batches pie filling of your choice

Sugar

EGG WASH

1 egg white plus 1 tablespoon (15 grams) water, fork beaten

PROCEDURE
· · · · ·

1. For a 12 × 17 × 1 inch (30 × 43 × 3 centimeters) size pan, roll out your dough in the shape of a rectangle about 15 × 20 inches (38 × 50 centimeters).
2. Fold the dough in half, and half again, so that your dough is now a quarter of its original size.
3. Place the center corner in the center of the baking pan. Then quickly and carefully unfold it to fill the bottom of the baking pan.
4. Place it in the freezer while you roll out the top crust for a full top, or cut lattice strips.
5. Make the filling of your choice and spread it out evenly in the pan.
6. Top the pie with the full top crust cut with some vents, or with

woven lattice strips that you have spliced together with a drop of water in order to make them extra long.

7. Neaten up the edges to about a 1-inch overhang and crimp.
8. Brush the pie with egg white wash.
9. Bake at 425°F (220°C) for 20 minutes. Lower the heat to 375°F (190°C), sprinkle with sugar, and bake for 25 to 30 minutes more until the crust is golden and the filling bubbly. Cool the pie for several hours before serving.

· · · · · · · · · OLD RECIPES WITH FEW DIRECTIONS · · · · · · · ·

My favorite pie recipe comes from *Home Economics* (1929), a thin, cardboard-covered, spiral-bound compilation of recipes edited by the housewives of the Wikiup Grange of Astoria, Oregon.

· · · · ·

"Line a pie tin with crust and fill with chopped apples,
teaspoon cinnamon and as much sugar as
apples require according to tartness. Dot with butter
and cover with top crust. Brush with milk and bake."
—Mrs. John Bell

· · · · ·

Little Tasties

Every pie maker has a name for them: pinwheels, dough cookies, roll-ups, roly-polys, and my personal favorite that one of my students shared with me, little kisses. They're the tiny tidbits made with leftover dough trimmings and most commonly filled with cinnamon and sugar. One Saturday I wrapped up a dozen and took them with me on my errands. First stop was the recycling center, where I shared them with other town folks. I guess I shouldn't have been surprised when I was asked what time I would be back the following week. You can make a lot of people happy when you hand them a freshly baked treat.

LITTLE TASTIES ARE MADE WITH DOUGH SCRAPS, AND THE YIELD WILL BE
DIFFERENT EVERY TIME AND WITH EVERY PIE MAKER

INGREDIENTS
· · · · ·

Dough scraps

Sugar

Cinnamon

EGG WASH

1 egg white plus 1 tablespoon (15 grams) water, fork beaten

PROCEDURE
· · · · ·

1. Gather up your dough trimmings and, without kneading, gently push them together to form a ball.
2. On a floured surface roll out the dough in the shape of a rectangle.
3. Sprinkle a handful of sugar over the dough, leaving a ½-inch edge without sugar. Follow with a good amount of cinnamon, probably more than you think. If you are skimpy with the cinnamon, the "tas-

ties" are not as satisfying. Brush a small amount of water along one of the long edges. Starting with the dry edge, roll the dough up jelly-roll fashion. Turn it over so that the sealed edge is on the bottom.

4. Brush the roll with leftover egg white wash, or another wash of your choice (see Washes, page 56).

5. Cut the roll crosswise into approximately 1-inch (3 to 4 centimeters) pieces and place on a parchment-lined baking sheet. I use a ⅛-size sheet pan.

6. Bake for 15 minutes at 425°F (220°C). If your oven runs hot, check them earlier as they may be done sooner.

7. As soon as the tasties come out of the oven, sprinkle them liberally with sugar.

8. Let the tasties cool and enjoy.

VARIATIONS
· · · · ·

ALMOND TASTIES In a small bowl, mix together egg white wash, egg yolk, almond meal or flour, sugar, and spices, making a thick mixture. Spoon the mixture on your rolled dough and spread with a spatula, leaving a ½-inch (1.25 centimeters) edge. Finish as usual.

FLAVOR SUGGESTIONS Cinnamon, ground coffee, ground clove, chili powder, coconut, unsweetened cocoa powder, cocoa nibs, or make them savory with cheese and herbs.

Hand Pies and Jam Pies

When you come right down to it, eating something like a pie right out of hand is just darn fun. There is no recipe for the filling other than to use your own imagination. Less is definitely more when you are filling hand pies. For a small empanada-size pastry, I place only one raspberry, ⅓ teaspoon lemon curd, ⅛ teaspoon sugar, and a very tiny pinch of nutmeg—really just a few grains. Use a firm but not rough touch when using a dough press. The first time I used one, I whomped really hard on it, thinking it would seal the hand pie better, but most of the filling burst out of the dough and landed on the counter.

3-INCH PRESS YIELDS 24–32 HAND PIES; 4-INCH PRESS YIELDS ABOUT 22 HAND PIES

INGREDIENTS
· · · · ·

1 recipe double-crust pie dough

SUGGESTED FILLINGS

Lemon curd (see page 133)

Mincemeat

Mascarpone cheese

Orange marmalade

Homemade jam

Raspberries, blueberries, blackberries

Apple pie filling

Pecans or other nuts (candied is nice)

Chocolate bits

Cinnamon, nutmeg, or other spices you like

EGG WASH

1 egg white plus 1 tablespoon (15 grams) water, fork beaten

CONTINUED

PROCEDURE

. . . . .

1. Roll out the dough on a pastry cloth, parchment paper, or well-floured surface.

2. Using round, square, or rectangle dough presses, cut out as many shapes as you can.

3. If using a dough press, open it and place a bit of flour on the surface before placing the dough on top of it.

4. Put a scant teaspoon or less of the filling mix of your choice on one half of the dough. Add more if you are using a larger dough press. Brush the edge with a tiny bit of water, and press firmly to make a seal.

5. Take a fork or knife and poke a little vent on top.

6. Cover and chill the hand pies for a few minutes until you are ready to bake, or freeze them for baking another time.

7. When you are ready to bake, preheat the oven to 400°F (205°C). Brush the hand pies lightly with an egg wash and sprinkle them with a bit of sugar.

8. Bake the pies for 10 to 15 minutes, then let them cool and enjoy.

. . . . · NOTES · . . . .

For a savory version, try greens and garlic sautéed in olive oil, mixed with feta or blue cheese, and leave the sprinkle of sugar off. If you don't have a dough press, take a tuna-fish can, cut out the top and bottom with a can opener and you have an instant form to use.

. . . .

Lemon Curd

8 tablespoons (112 grams) butter, salted

1 cup (200 grams) sugar

Zest of 4 lemons, chopped fine

Juice of 4 lemons

4 eggs and 2 egg yolks, beaten

PROCEDURE

· · · · ·

1. In a medium saucepan, melt the butter on low.
2. Add the sugar, then the lemon zest, lemon juice, and eggs, in that order.
3. Over low heat, stir the mixture gently until it thickens enough to coat the back of a wooden spoon without running off.
4. Remove the mixture from the heat and let it cool, then refrigerate it.

Pie Pops

These are fun, easy, and very cute. Lollipop sticks can be found in craft stores, in some baking sections, and online.

3-INCH PRESS YIELDS 12-16 PIE POPS

INGREDIENTS
· · · · ·

1 recipe double-crust pie dough

Fillings as suggested in Hand Pies (see page 131)

EGG WASH

1 egg white plus 1 tablespoon (15 grams) water, fork beaten

PROCEDURE
· · · · ·

1. Roll out the dough and cut 3-inch (7.5 centimeters) dough circles with a floured dough press or cookie cutter.
2. Spoon 2 teaspoons of filling into the center of half of the circles.
3. Place a lollipop stick onto the dough so that the end sticks out several inches and press firmly down, but not so hard that the stick goes all the way through the dough.
4. Lightly wet the edges of the dough circle, place another dough circle on top, and press the edges together with a fork crimp. Be sure to close the dough around the stick. Prick lightly once with a fork or make 4 or 5 vents with a toothpick.
5. Place the pie pop on a parchment-covered baking tray. Cover and chill for a few minutes until you are ready to bake, or freeze them.
6. When you are ready to bake, preheat the oven to 400°F (205°C). Brush the pie pops lightly with an egg wash and sprinkle them with a bit of sugar.
7. Bake the pie pops for 10 to 15 minutes, then let them cool and enjoy.

Rustic Tart

In France, these are known as gallettes; in Italy, crostata. The amount and kind of filling you put inside doesn't have to be exact.

MAKES 2 TARTS

INGREDIENTS
· · · · ·

1 recipe double-crust pie dough

½ recipe apple, pear, or cranberry pie filling; or 4 cups fresh fruit

¼ cup sugar, if using fresh fruit, plus extra

Small grating of fresh nutmeg, if using fresh fruit

EGG WASH

1 egg white plus 1 tablespoon (15 grams) water, fork beaten

PROCEDURE
· · · · ·

1. Roll the dough out to about 14 inches (35 centimeters) in diameter and about ¼-inch (.6-centimeter) thick and place on a parchment-covered sheet pan or cookie tin.
2. Spread pie filling or place fresh fruit in the middle of the dough, leaving a 2- to 3-inch (5- to 7-centimeter) border. Sprinkle the fresh fruit evenly with sugar and nutmeg.
3. Fold the edges of the dough up and over the filling and overlap, leaving an opening in the center.
4. Chill in the fridge or freezer for 30 minutes until the dough is firm. Preheat the oven to 425°F (220°C).
5. Lightly brush some of the egg white wash over the edges, and sprinkle with some extra sugar.
6. Bake for 10 minutes, then turn the oven down to 375°F (190°C) and bake for 30 minutes more, until golden brown.

Fried Pies

My friend Jennifer and I were demonstrating different types of pie making at a farmers' market one afternoon in late summer. I made a peach pie and Jennifer made her delicious fried pies with blackberry filling. She says: "These are good at room temperature, but I encourage you to organize your life around having at least one while still warm. Or kind of wreck the first one, so you'll be forced to eat it, lest you serve something unsightly to a guest. Hospitality requires it, you know." I couldn't agree more. The quince and blackberry fillings are from Jennifer, and the peach filling is from me. The very tender dough is closer to what one makes for a biscuit, and lard makes it easy to work. I'm sorry to say that gluten-free flour does not work for this one. You'll have some extra quince filling left for adding a half-cup or so to an apple or pear pie filling for a little surprise.

MAKES ABOUT 12 FRIED PIES

INGREDIENTS
· · · · ·

1 batch pie filling of your choice (recipes follow)

1 batch Jennifer's Fried Pie Dough (see page 68)

Additional flour for rolling out dough

1 cup (224 grams) or more of leaf lard for frying

½ cup (100 grams) sugar

PROCEDURE (FOR THE PIES)

·····

1. Make the filling of your choice.
2. On a floured board, lightly roll each circle of dough into about a 5-inch (12- to 13-centimeter) circle.
3. Place a soup spoon's worth of filling in the center of each circle.
4. Moisten the edges of the dough with your fingertip and water, then fold over gently (careful not to tear the dough), and seal all the edges completely.
5. Crimp the edges with a fork. Brush off any extra flour. Continue with the rest of the dough.

FRY

·····

1. Put 1 cup (224 grams) of leaf lard in a wide steep-sided skillet, and heat until a tiny ball of dough sizzles mightily when dropped in it.
2. Gently lay the pies in, without crowding, a few at a time.
3. Fry the pies in batches until they are golden, then turn them gently and fry the other side. You may have to stand them upright, too, to get an all-over gold. Add more lard as necessary.
4. Remove the fried pies and immediately place them on a plate of sugar, turning quickly to lightly coat all sides, or sprinkle lightly and evenly on all sides. If you get too much sugar on, you can brush off the extra with a pastry brush.
5. Place the pies on a rack to cool.

Quince Filling

INGREDIENTS
· · · · ·

5 quince, peeled, cored, and diced

About 1 cup (200 grams) sugar (depends on how astringent the quince are)

Water

1 knife tip (1 small pinch) ground cloves

2 knife tips (2 small pinches) ground cinnamon

1 tablespoon (15 grams) freshly squeezed lemon juice

1 teaspoon vanilla or the scrapings of a vanilla bean

3 tablespoons (42 grams) butter

PROCEDURE
· · · · ·

1. Place the fruit and sugar in a saucepan with just enough water to cover them.
2. Bring the water to a boil and then lower the heat to a simmer.
3. Add the spices and lemon juice.
4. Stew the fruit over low heat until it is soft, but still a bit chunky, and most of the liquid has cooked away.
5. At the very end, stir in the vanilla and butter.
6. Let the mixture cool. (If you make this ahead and refrigerate, bring back to room temperature before using.)

Blackberry Filling

INGREDIENTS
· · · · ·

2 pints ripe blackberries

⅔ cup (66 grams) sugar

1 grating fresh nutmeg

2 knife tips ground cinnamon (optional)

PROCEDURE
· · · · ·

Put all the ingredients into a bowl and lightly mix.

Peach Filling

INGREDIENTS
· · · · ·

2–3 sweet ripe peaches, cut into small pieces

1 grating nutmeg

1 tablespoon (12 grams) sugar, or more according to taste

Small pinch of salt

¼ teaspoon (1 gram) freshly squeezed lemon juice

1 teaspoon (5 grams) orange liqueur (optional)

PROCEDURE
· · · · ·

Put all the ingredients into a bowl and lightly mix.

CHAPTER THREE

The Quintessential Apple Pie

The big garden from which I fed my young family

had soil rich in nutrients, so it was easy to grow nearly anything. Not so at the little cottage I moved to in town. What I found there was dirt that needed care and feeding and the tenacious roots of field grass that spread everywhere. Computers were new in our lives at that time, and, although I saw myself as a Luddite who would hold the line against the soulless machines, when Duncan's grandpa gave us one purely for homeschooling purposes I couldn't help but poke around on it, too.

I soon came across an active composting forum that seemed just right for asking a question about mulching away the grass. Within minutes of posting I received a response from a serious organic garden devotee, who offered to give me the "nickel tour" of some active mulches in the vegetable beds he tended at a community garden in Seattle. When I responded, "I don't do Seattle," he offered to drive the three hours west to help me get a mulch started in my own front yard.

On the appointed day, he arrived with buckets full of coffee grounds, juice pulp, burlap coffee sacks, and bags of leaves that he pulled from the trunk of his car. I immediately nicknamed him the "Mulchman," and he regularly returned to check on the project. Under the cover of a deep burlap-covered mulch, the field grass did greatly decrease, leaving me with well-nourished soil just as he had predicted; eight months later, in the summer, I had the beginnings of a sweet cottage garden with thriving vegetables planted between a riot of brightly colored flowers.

Over the months of soil building, I increasingly looked forward to his visits. But it wasn't until he spread pink rose petals up and down my garden path that I realized he was courting me . . . with mulch. Like the garden, our relationship thrived; so much so that twelve months after we met online we were engaged, and married a year later.

After we had been married for a few years, he asked me if I would make him an apple pie. No need to ask twice—of course I would, and since I wanted it to be the best apple pie he had ever had, an unexpected project was born that was a perfect pairing of our individual talents: I made the pies, and he ate them. Of course he gave feedback, which I dutifully sifted through, using some but not all of his suggestions in true wifely fashion. During the apple harvest time, I looked forward to weekend visits to local farmers' markets where artisan growers proudly offered tastes of apples with names I had never heard of, like Arkansas Black, Belle de Boskoop, and Bramley's Seedling. Until starting this weekly practice, I had no idea that there could be so many different varieties, or that the addition of just one especially sweet Egremont Russet could boost a pie's flavor from simply good to incredibly great.

Returning home with a cornucopia of apple varieties (enough to fill up one entire refrigerator) I'd head right into the kitchen, and the experiments were on. I created fillings made from the day's treasures, and with ever-changing amounts of sugar, spicing, additions of artisan apple cider vinegar, or a French calvados (apple brandy), I mounded them mile-high in a pie pan. After the finished pie was cool enough for tasting, I would bring the Mulchman a slice. I made a pie a day, and often more than one, and we dutifully tasted our way straight through to the following weekend, when the pro-cess would begin again. Making "The Quintessential Apple Pie" was a joyous quest to which we both contributed.

Author Malcom Gladwell, in his book *Outliers*, says it takes roughly ten thousand hours of practice in a field to achieve mastery. More than anything, the hundreds of pies I created in my sunny kitchen, over many happy hours, helped me to hone my pie-making skills, the results of which were shared with friends, family, and, of course, the Mulchman. "The way to a man's heart is through his stomach" were words that I had heard both my grandmother and mom say on many occasions when I was growing up. To reach the Mulchman's heart, I made pies infused with love from mine.

A TART SWEET MIX OF MANY APPLES MAKES A GREAT PIE

Heirloom apples are showing up more regularly at farmers' markets. Newtown Pippin, Golden Russet, Bramley's Seedling, and Spitzenberg are a few varieties that will make some very flavorful pies. Each region of the country will grow specific varieties, too. Rowan Jacobsen's excellent book, *Apples of Uncommon Character*, features 123 different varieties of apples, complete with their flavor profiles and baking properties—a real boon to the pie baker. You may not find all of these at your farmers' market, but here are some varieties I use in my apple pie fillings.

Arkansas Black	Tart and crisp (November)
Ashmead's Kernel	Tart, juicy, and crisp, with a slightly sweet pear flavor (November)
Baldwin	Tart and holds its shape (October)
Belle de Boskoop	Tart and holds its shape (October)
Black Twig	Tart, spicy, and firm (October)
Bramley's Seedling	Tart and crisp (October)
Cox's Orange Pippin	Sweet and tender (September/October)
Egremont Russet	Sweet and firm (October)
Golden Russet	Sweet, tart, spicy, and firm (October)
Gravenstein	Tart, sweet, and tender (August)
Elstar	Sweet and tender (October)
Empire	Sweet and tender (September)
Esopus Spitzenberg	Bright, acidic, sweet, juicy, and crisp (October)
Holstein	Sweet and tart, crisp and juicy (October)
Jonathan	Tart and spicy, juicy, and tender (October)
King David	Spicy and crisp (October)
Macoun	Sweet, tart, and tender (October)
McIntosh	Spicy, tart, and tender (September)

Melrose	Sweet and holds its shape (September/October)
Newtown Pippin	Tart, firm, crisp, and juicy; holds its shape and keeps well (October/November)
Northern Spy	Sweet, tart, juicy, and firm (November)
Prairie Spy	Sweet and firm (October)
Rome	Tart and firm, but can get mushy (October)
Roxbury Russet	Tart, crisp, and dense (September)
Rubinette	Tart and holds its shape (October)
Smokehouse	Sweet, with a cider flavor (September/October)
Spartan	Sweet and crisp (October)
Spigold	Sweet, spicy, and firm (October)
Stayman Winesap	Tart and spicy, crisp and tender (October)
Tompkin's King	Sweet, tart, and juicy (October)

· · · · · · · · · · APPLES AT THE STORE · · · · · · · · · ·

Here are some notes on the flavor and texture of grocery store varietals. Buy organic whenever possible and ask the produce manager or greengrocer for a taste to consider if the fruit is "pie worthy."

Braeburn	Slightly tart
Cameo	Slightly sweet and tart, soft
Fuji	Sweet and crisp
Gala	Mild, sweet, and crisp,
Golden Delicious	Sweet and soft
Granny Smith	Tart and crisp
Honeycrisp	Sweet and tart, crisp and juicy
Jazz	Sweet, crisp, and juicy
Pink Lady	Tart and sweet, firm and crisp
Red Delicious	Mildly sweet, mushy, and doesn't bake well

After Duncan headed off to college, I moved from my cottage to share a house with the Mulchman in Seattle. With lovely oak floors, arched doorways, tall ceilings, and big southwest-facing windows that let in tons of beautiful light, the house must have been lovely when young, but now in her eighties she was showing definite signs of wear. Friendly neighbors on all sides made it easier to overlook the lack of insulation, an aging woodstove, and "Methuselah," which is what I had silently named the ancient and very expensive oil-fueled furnace that clanged and banged when in use. The cheery 1920s kitchen, with original yellow and white tile on the counters and back splashes, tall cupboards, and breakfast nook still intact, was where I spent many happy hours baking. It was at these counters that I spent over two years learning about pie dough, and sharing the results of my explorations. In time, word began to get around that I was making some pretty good pies, and I was asked if I might be willing to teach a class. I've always loved to teach, so a date was set for three aspiring pie makers to join me.

I was just pulling an apple pie out of the oven when they arrived, which put everyone in the right mood for baking. We put on aprons and set to work to make three more. My floury hands guided us through the dough and filling, and we laughed while rolling, chopping, sweetening, and seasoning our apples. When all the pies were tucked into the oven to bake, we collapsed in overstuffed chairs with big smiles on our faces. My just baked pie was still warm, so I cut slices to share. Between mouthfuls, I answered as many questions as I could on technique, pie lore, and history.

We didn't need an oven timer to let us know our pies were ready, because the scent that was wafting through the entire house was nearly intoxicating.

We gathered in the kitchen, and one by one we pulled out three golden brown, steaming hot pies to exclamations of "I can't believe I made this!" "It's so beautiful." "I'm sharing this with my family tonight." This is pie love, a moment when pie makers only have eyes for their pies. I have seen it at every workshop since this first one. A "graduation picture" was taken, and after they left, I felt that I just might have stumbled into a new and unexpected career teaching pie making. A few days later, I set up a rudimentary website and was astounded when workshops started to fill almost immediately. This was enough to make me feel I should keep going and see where the pie-way would lead me next.

Teaching pie making is not all that different from what I had learned in decades of my first career as a music teacher. First you present the finished piece for the student to hear and be inspired by—in this case, a freshly baked pie to see, smell and taste. Break the work down into small achievable sections: dough, filling, rolling, finishing, and baking. Encourage and motivate along the way. Gently and with good humor, shine a light on ways to make each task easier. Give easy to remember word pictures that encourage pie makers to be in charge of their dough and not the other way around. "Flip that dough over just like you would a wet wash cloth." "Let the dough ease down into the pan like you are covering a sleeping baby." Finally, always keep your eye on the big picture: Pie! After teaching hundreds of workshops all over the country, every session is unique and I continue to learn something new each time. I can't imagine any other work being more creative, fun, and meaningful than this.

The Quintessential Apple Pie

I don't peel apples as most skins become soft in the baking, plus their tannins add flavor to the pie. If there is an apple with skin you find too thick, it's just "off with their jackets!" as Henry Ward Beecher wrote. A mix of six to eight different varieties, some for tart, some that hold their shape, and some that don't, will give you a pie with exceptional flavor and texture.

MAKES ONE 9-INCH DEEP-DISH PIE

INGREDIENTS
· · · · ·

About 10 cups heritage apples (skin on), quartered and cored, to mound up high in the pie pan

½ cup (100 grams) sugar

½ teaspoon (3 grams) salt

1 teaspoon (2 grams) cinnamon

2 gratings nutmeg

½ teaspoon (1 gram) allspice

1 tablespoon (12 grams) artisan apple cider vinegar or 1–2 teaspoons (5–10 grams) freshly squeezed lemon juice

1–2 tablespoons (15–30 grams) calvados or other apple liqueur (optional but really good)

½ cup (73 grams) flour

1 recipe double-crust pie dough

1 knob butter, the size of a small walnut, cut into small pieces for dotting the top of the filling

1–2 teaspoons (4–8 grams) sugar, for sprinkling on top of the pie

EGG WASH

1 egg white plus 1 tablespoon (15 grams) water, fork beaten

CONTINUED

PROCEDURE

· · · · ·

1. Slice the apples into ½-inch (1.5 centimeters) thick slices, or chunk them up into pieces you can comfortably get into your mouth.

2. In a large mixing bowl, put the apples, sugar, salt, cinnamon, nutmeg, allspice, vinegar, calvados, and flour, and mix lightly until most of the surfaces are covered with what looks like wet sand.

3. Pour the mixture into an unbaked piecrust, mounding high, and dot with butter.

4. Roll out the remaining dough, lay it over the fruit, and cut 5 to 6 vents on top. Trim the excess dough from the edges and crimp (see Vents, Appliqués, Crimps, Flutes, Lattice, pages 51–56).

5. Cover the pie and chill in refrigerator while you preheat the oven to 425°F (220°C).

6. Lightly brush some of the egg white wash over the entire pie, including the edges, and bake on the middle rack of the oven for 20 minutes.

7. Reduce the heat to 375°F (190°C) and bake for 30 minutes longer.

8. Open the oven and carefully sprinkle sugar evenly on top of the pie, then continue baking for 10 minutes more.

9. Look for steam and a slight bit of juice coming out of the vents before removing the pie from the oven. Get your ear right down almost to the top of the pie and listen for the sizzle-whump, which some call the pie's heartbeat (see Kate's Very Short Glossary of Pie-Making Terms on page 333).

10. Cool the pie for at least an hour.

VARIATIONS

· · · · ·

APPLE CHEDDAR PIE Make this pie with either of the cheddar cheese crusts (page 63 or 86 for gluten-free). Or add up to 1 cup grated cheese to the filling, or fill the pie halfway, top with sliced cheese, and spoon in remainder of filling.

LEMON VS. VINEGAR

Many baking books include a squeeze of lemon in the ingredients list for fruit pie, which gives the filling a bright note, but for apple pies I switch it up. This started on a day when I didn't have any lemon in the house, and quite frankly, I didn't want to take the car out for this one little thing. So, what to use? I opened up the door to my baking cupboard and spied an unopened bottle of an artisan apple cider vinegar purchased months earlier at a farmers' market. "Apples to apples," I said, and measured out one tablespoon to sprinkle over the rest of the ingredients in the bowl. The results, after baking? Well, those who had tasted my apple pies before thought that the flavor of this filling was better than those made with lemon, and I thought so, too. Look for a good artisan apple cider vinegar at your farmers' market, or Bragg's Apple Cider Vinegar at the grocery store. Heinz cider vinegar is not an acceptable substitution, as its acidity is too refined for good flavor. In a pinch you can always put in a squeeze of lemon.

· · · · · PRE-COOKING AND FREEZING APPLE PIE FILLING · · · · ·

Apples slump when they are baked, and this can leave a gap between the filling and the top crust. I call this the Grand Canyon. I don't mind this gap at all, but if this isn't how you like to slice your pie, then try pre-cooking the filling in a braising pan on medium-low heat for about 15 minutes, just until the juices start to flow. Don't cook the filling all the way through. When a fork begins to easily pierce a piece, then pull the pan from the heat and let the filling cool completely before placing it in a well-chilled pie shell. Top with the upper crust, finish as usual, and bake. Since the apples have already done their slump, you won't find the big gap anymore.

You can also take the partially cooked apple pie filling one step further, so you can use it later. After the filling has cooled, spoon it into freezer bags that you have dated and labeled, and place them in the freezer. When the urge to make pie strikes you, make your dough, and about 15 to 20 minutes before you are going to roll it out, pull a bag of your frozen pre-cooked filling from the freezer and set it on the counter to partially thaw. Don't thaw it all the way, but just enough so it can go into an unbaked pie shell without being a frozen block. Spread the filling around evenly in the pie shell and make a small mound in the middle. Dot the filling with butter, roll out the top crust, place it on top of the semi-frozen filling, seal the edges, and crimp. Don't forget to cut a few vents. Add an extra 10 to 15 minutes to your usual bake time. This is great to do with apples that don't store well, like early season Gravensteins. Their wonderful tart and sweet balance is an unexpected treat in the winter and spring.

· ·

Apple Cranberry Walnut Pie

Adding just a cup of walnuts and another of cranberries makes this pie a seasonal variation on the classic apple pie theme. The cranberries add nice red color highlights to the filling, too.

MAKES ONE 9-INCH DEEP-DISH PIE

INGREDIENTS

· · · · ·

8 cups heritage apples (skin on), quartered and cored

1 cup (99 grams) cranberries, fresh or unthawed frozen

1 cup (120 grams) chopped walnuts

⅔ cup (133 grams) sugar

½ teaspoon (3 grams) salt

1 (2 grams) teaspoon cinnamon

2 gratings nutmeg

½ teaspoon (1 gram) allspice

1 tablespoon (12 grams) an artisan apple cider vinegar or 1–2 teaspoons (5–10 grams) freshly squeezed lemon juice

1–2 tablespoons (15–30 grams) calvados or other apple liqueur (optional but really good)

½ cup (73 grams) flour

1 recipe double-crust pie dough

1 knob butter, the size of a small walnut, cut into small pieces for dotting the top of the filling

1–2 teaspoons (4–8 grams) sugar, for sprinkling on top of the pie

EGG WASH

1 egg white plus 1 tablespoon (15 grams) water, fork beaten

PROCEDURE

· · · · ·

1. Slice the apples into ½-inch (1.5-centimeter) thick slices, or chunk them up into pieces you can comfortably get into your mouth.

2. In a large mixing bowl, put the apples, cranberries, walnuts, sugar, salt, cinnamon, nutmeg, allspice, vinegar, calvados, and flour, and mix lightly until most of the surfaces are covered with what looks like wet sand.

3. Pour the mixture into an unbaked piecrust, mounding high, and dot with butter.

4. Roll out the remaining dough, lay it over the fruit, and cut 5 to 6 vents on top. Trim the excess dough from the edges and crimp (see Vents, Appliqués, Crimps, Flutes, Lattice, pages 51–56).

5. Cover the pie and chill in refrigerator while you preheat the oven to 425°F (220°C).

6. Lightly brush some of the egg white wash over the entire pie, including the edges, and bake on middle rack of oven for 20 minutes.

7. Reduce the heat to 375°F (190°C) and bake for 30 minutes longer.

8. Open the oven and carefully sprinkle on sugar evenly on top, then continue baking for 10 minutes more.

9. Look for steam and a slight bit of juice coming out of the vents before removing the pie from the oven. Get your ear right down almost to the top of the pie and listen for the sizzle-whump, which some also call the pie's heartbeat (see Kate's Very Short Glossary of Pie-Making Terms on page 333).

10. Cool the pie for at least an hour before eating.

Apple Quince Pie

Decades ago, a quince tree used to be common in home gardens. The yellow fruit is larger than an apple and slightly misshapen. It is highly astringent and not great for out of hand eating. Adding just one diced-up quince to an apple or pear pie is bound to get friends asking you just what that exotic flavor is that they can't quite put their finger on. Look for quince in farmers' markets and grocery produce sections in the fall. Set one to ripen on your kitchen windowsill and enjoy the heady fragrance it sends through the house.

MAKES ONE 9-INCH DEEP-DISH PIE

INGREDIENTS
. . . . .

8 cups heritage apples (skin on), quartered and cored

1 quince (skin on), quartered, cored

½ cup (100 grams) sugar

½ teaspoon (3 grams) salt

1 teaspoon (2 grams) cinnamon

2 gratings nutmeg

½ teaspoon (1 gram) allspice

1 tablespoon (12 grams) an artisan apple cider vinegar or 1–2 teaspoons (5–10 grams) freshly squeezed lemon juice

1–2 tablespoons (15–30 grams) calvados or other apple liqueur (optional but really good)

½ cup (73 grams) flour

1 recipe double-crust pie dough

1 knob butter, the size of a small walnut, cut into small pieces for dotting the top of the filling

1–2 teaspoons (4–8 grams) sugar, for sprinkling on top of the pie

EGG WASH

1 egg white plus 1 tablespoon (15 grams) water, fork beaten

PROCEDURE

· · · · ·

1. Slice apples into ½-inch (1.5-centimeter) thick slices, or chunk them up into pieces you can comfortably get into your mouth. Cut and dice the quince into smaller pieces than the apples so they will mix through the filling well.

2. In a large mixing bowl, put the apples, quince, sugar, salt, cinnamon, nutmeg, allspice, vinegar, calvados, and flour, and mix lightly until most of the surfaces are covered with what looks like wet sand.

3. Pour the mixture into an unbaked piecrust, mounding high, and dot with butter.

4. Roll out the remaining dough, lay it over the fruit, and cut 5 to 6 vents on top. Trim the excess dough from the edges and crimp (see Vents, Appliqués, Crimps, Flutes, Lattice, pages 51–56).

5. Cover the pie and chill in refrigerator while you preheat the oven to 425°F (220°C).

6. Lightly brush some of the egg white wash over the entire pie, including the edges, and bake on middle rack of oven for 20 minutes.

7. Reduce the heat to 375°F (190°C) and bake for 30 minutes longer.

8. Open the oven and carefully sprinkle sugar evenly on top, then continue baking for 10 minutes more.

9. Look for steam and a slight bit of juice coming out of the vents before removing the pie from the oven. Get your ear right down almost to the top of the pie and listen for the sizzle-whump, which some also call the pie's heartbeat (see Kate's Very Short Glossary of Pie-Making Terms on page 333).

10. Cool the pie for at least an hour before eating.

Pear Pie

Pear pies and apple pies share many similarities. Just as I do for apple pies, I leave my pears unpeeled and mound them high in the pie shell. Sweetener and thickener amounts are similar, and the artisan apple cider vinegar works very well in pear pies, just as it does with apple. Pears ripen from the inside out, so if you aren't going to use them right away, store them in the fridge until a day or so before you are ready to use them. When ripe, you should feel a slight give around the stem. For this recipe, if you can get your hands on some Warren pears, you'll love the vanilla undercurrent. Bosc, Comice, D'Anjou—really any combination of pears will make this delicious fall pie.

MAKES ONE 9-INCH DEEP-DISH PIE

INGREDIENTS
. . . . .

7–8 pears (skin on), quartered and cored

½ cup (73 grams) flour

½ cup (100 grams) sugar

½ teaspoon (3 grams) salt

1 teaspoon (2 grams) cinnamon

2 gratings nutmeg

½ teaspoon (1 gram) allspice

1 tablespoon (15 grams) pear vinegar or an artisan apple cider vinegar

1–2 tablespoons (15–30 grams) pear brandy, optional

1 recipe double-crust pie dough

2 teaspoons (9 grams) butter, chopped into little pieces

1–2 teaspoons (4–8 grams) sugar, for sprinkling on top of the pie

EGG WASH

1 egg white mixed with 1 tablespoon (15 grams) water, fork-beaten

CONTINUED

PROCEDURE

· · · · ·

1. Slice pears into ½-inch (1.5-centimeter) slices or chunk them up into pieces you can comfortably get into your mouth.

2. In a large mixing bowl, place all the ingredients, except the butter, and mix lightly until most of the surfaces are covered.

3. Pour the mixture into an unbaked piecrust, mounding high, and dot with butter.

4. Roll out the remaining dough, lay it over the fruit, and cut 5 to 6 vents on top. Trim the excess dough from the edges and crimp (see Vents, Appliqués, Crimps, Flutes, Lattice, pages 51–56).

5. Cover the pie and chill in refrigerator while you preheat the oven to 425°F (220°C).

6. Lightly brush some of the egg white wash over the entire pie, including the edges, and bake on the middle rack of the oven for 20 minutes.

7. Reduce the heat to 375°F (190°C) and bake for 30 minutes longer.

8. Open the oven and carefully sprinkle sugar evenly on top, then continue baking for 10 minutes more.

9. Look for steam and a slight bit of juice coming out of the vents before removing the pie from the oven. Get your ear right down almost to the top of the pie and listen for the sizzle-whump, which some also call the pie's heartbeat (see Kate's Very Short Glossary of Pie-Making Terms on page 333).

10. Cool the pie for at least an hour before eating.

VARIATIONS

· · · · ·

PEAR QUINCE PIE Replace 1 pear with 1 quince, chopped up into small pieces no larger than almonds.

PEAR WALNUT PIE Add 1 cup (120 grams) walnuts

PEAR CRANBERRY PIE Add 1 cup (99 grams) whole cranberries, fresh or unthawed frozen

PEAR CRANBERRY WALNUT PIE Add 1 cup (99 grams) whole cranberries and 1 cup (120 grams) walnuts

Poached Pear Sour Cream Caramel Pie with a Crumb Topping

Poached pear pie has always been a much-anticipated treat in our family and on 3.14.15, called "Pi Day of the Century," we created a new version with layers of poached pears, caramel sauce, sweetened sour cream, and an oat-crisp topping. After it cooled, we served it to eagerly awaiting family and friends right at 9:26 p.m., the next three digits in pi.

MAKES ONE 9-INCH DEEP-DISH PIE

INGREDIENTS

. . . . .

1 recipe single-crust pie dough

1 recipe Crumble Topping (see page 95)

2½ pounds (1.1 kilograms) pears, ripe but slightly firm

4 cups (946 grams) apple juice

⅓ cup (33 grams) sugar

1 tablespoon (15 grams) freshly squeezed lemon juice

½ cup (118 grams) whipping cream

1½ cups (368 grams) sour cream

¼ cup (36 grams) flour

½ cup (100 grams) sugar

½ teaspoon powdered ground ginger

CONTINUED

PROCEDURE

. . . . .

1. Roll out the bottom dough and place it in your pie pan. Trim the excess dough from the edges and crimp. Cover the pan with plastic and place it in your refrigerator to chill. Make sure your crumble topping is also chilling in the freezer.
2. Peel, quarter, and core the pears, and then set them aside.
3. In a non-corrosive braising pan, simmer the apple juice, sugar, and lemon juice for 10 minutes.
4. Add the pears and simmer until they're soft, about 20 minutes. Remove the pears from the pan and set them aside to cool.
5. Turn the heat up and reduce the remaining juice by half.
6. Add whipping cream and stand back, as it will bubble up!
7. Cook for a minute or two more and remove the pan from the heat while it is still sauce and before it becomes caramel.
8. In a small bowl, mix sour cream, flour, sugar, and ground ginger. Set the mixture aside.

TO ASSEMBLE

. . . . .

1. Arrange the poached pears in the bottom of the pie pan.
2. Drizzle the caramel sauce over the pears.
3. Spoon the sour cream mixture evenly over the caramel sauce.

TO BAKE

. . . . .

1. Bake in a preheated 400°F (205°C) oven for 25 minutes.
2. Open the oven and evenly spread the crumb topping over the sour cream, and continue baking for an additional 20 minutes.
3. Remove the pie from the oven and place on a cooling rack. Serve slightly warm.

CHAPTER FOUR

A Berry Pie for Julia

Since the Mulchman had given me the nickel tour

of his garden beds in Seattle, I thought it would be a fun surprise to return the favor and give him the tour of Santa Barbara, the beautiful town where I had grown up. I wanted to share with him the scent of night-blooming jasmine, the sight of jacaranda trees dressed in their beautiful purple blooms like ladies going to a fancy tea, and the soft ocean breeze that almost, but not quite, was replicated on late summer evenings at my Pie Cottage home. There was another reason for going. I had made arrangements for us to have lunch with Julia Child. On the appointed day and hour, I navigated the winding lanes of Montecito to Casa Dorinda, which when I was growing up was known as the Bliss Estate. When we arrived, Julia opened her door, saying, "Welcome, dears. Come see my new digs." Her voice, so warm and welcoming, was just like I imagined it would be. I was meeting the doyenne of French cooking in America, and chatting with her as if we had known each other for years. After a quick tour of her "digs" she suggested we go to Moby Dick, a restaurant on Stearns Wharf that I had been to many times before.

My family has a very long Santa Barbara history, but until that day, I didn't realize that Julia did, too. She seemed genuinely interested in some of the little known bits of history and local lore that I knew, and vice versa. For one, the restaurant we were lunching in used to be the greasy spoon hangout for the local fishermen, owned by my late godfather. As a teenager, Moby Dick was a place I spent countless hours drinking coffee, sharing big ideas and deep thoughts with friends as we watched brown pelicans dive into the water in search of tasty tidbits off Stearns Wharf. Over our meal, Julia and I listed other places nearby that were mutually important to us. We chatted. We laughed. We lunched. She spread incredible amounts of butter on her oyster crackers. As we got up from the table, she asked if I might be kind enough to drive her to some of her favorite places "one last time." I brought the car around and helped her into the front seat, and we set off for our first stop, the Morton Bay Fig Tree near the train station, just a few blocks up from the beach. We took the time to get out and read the plaque placed under its branches. Legend has it that a sailor gave the seed of this tree to a Spanish girl he loved. We remarked that it must have been quite some kind of love, because hundreds of years later it is still growing and providing shade to those who gather under its branches. Butterfly Beach was next, and she pointed out the location where her family summer home had been, almost the very same spot where my family loved to watch the sun set behind the Channel Islands. Then on to Montecito Shores, which is part of the old Hammond Estate (if you know Santa Barbara history). This was the last place Julia lived with her beloved husband, Paul, up until his death in 1994. The guard at the gatehouse recognized Julia immediately, and she him. A few pleasantries shared, and we passed through the gates while she navigated us through the twisting lanes to a spot where we could best view her West Coast home. She said that Paul and she had spent a lot of money to live there but were "very happy being so close to the sea, so it was worth it."

We drove back to her home, helped her inside, and continued chatting on her shaded patio. As the afternoon was passing by quickly now, she took my hands and said, "Please, come back to see me, dear." I had every intention in the world of doing just that. We said our farewells, and after hugs and kisses, off we went. Every month that would go by I felt Julia's words tugging at me, and tried to find the time to carve out just a few days from work to see her.

In August of 2004, a mutual long-time friend of Julia's was staying at my cottage for a few days. As we were picking up a salmon for that night's dinner, the woman behind the counter said to us, "Did you hear that Julia Child passed away?" The news was startling, and we were both speechless for a moment. Although I had met Julia only once, I felt the hours of that one special visit to have been precious and meaningful. In unison, we asked, "When?" "I just heard it on the news" she said, and handed us our fish. The local radio news was playing in the background, and we stopped and listened, to see if we would hear the words about her, about Julia. We headed the few blocks up the hill to my cottage in stunned silence. As the afternoon went on, we prepared the meal for the evening. I wove my first lattice top crust on a blackberry pie, thinking of her as I carefully placed each strip on top of the shiny black fruit. With greens from my garden we made a salad, poached the salmon, chilled the wine, and even managed to maneuver my dining table on to the little deck that looks up to the mountains of Hurricane Ridge. It felt only right to add one more place for Julia. So on August 13, 2004, as the sun set on that last long summer evening of her life, gathered with family and friends, we toasted Julia's life, her love, her passion, and the legacy that she had left to all of us. Bon Appétit, Julia.

Blackberry Pie

Blackberries can be found across the country and ripen at the same time peaches do. Be sure to wear a long-sleeve shirt when picking blackberries since vines with thorns are prickly. Look for berries that are plump and almost black. Only pick the berries that come off the stem easily. If you have to tug it off, it isn't ripe and won't be sweet enough. I like the flavor of the fruit to shine through, so I use less than a cup of sugar in this pie, but after the filling is made, taste it and add a bit more if you like it sweeter. This pie is beautiful when finished with a woven lattice top (see Vents, Appliqués, Crimps, Flutes, Lattice, pages 51 to 56). *Saveur Magazine* included my recipe in their 2008 *Saveur* 100 issue, along with its picture on the cover and centerfold.

MAKES ONE 9-INCH DEEP-DISH PIE

INGREDIENTS
· · · · ·

6 cups (680 grams), about 1½ pounds blackberries, fresh picked or unthawed frozen

¾ cup (150 grams) sugar

A small grating of freshly ground nutmeg

2 teaspoons (10 grams) freshly squeezed lemon juice and a few gratings of lemon zest

⅓ teaspoon (2 grams) salt

⅓ cup (48 grams) flour

½ teaspoon–1 tablespoon (2–12 grams) quick-cooking tapioca; add the larger amount if the berries are especially juicy

1 recipe double-crust pie dough

1 tablespoon (14 grams) butter

2 teaspoons (8 grams) sugar, for sprinkling on top of the pie

EGG WASH

1 egg white plus 1 tablespoon (15 grams) water, fork beaten

CONTINUED

PROCEDURE

· · · · ·

1. Preheat the oven to 425°F (220°C).
2. Put the blackberries, sugar, nutmeg, lemon juice, zest, salt, flour, and tapioca into a bowl and stir and fold until everything is evenly coated. Using the back of a wooden spoon, mash gently to make a textured filling.
3. Roll out the bottom dough and place it in your pie pan.
4. Pour the filling into the crust, dot it with butter, and set it aside.
5. Roll out the remaining dough, lay it over the fruit, trim, crimp, and cut 5 to 6 vents on top, or cut strips and weave a lattice top (see Vents, Appliqués, Crimps, Flutes, Lattice, pages 51–56).
6. Brush the crust with the egg white mixture.
7. Bake at 425°F (220°C) on the middle rack of the oven until the crust is golden brown, about 15 to 20 minutes. Reduce the heat to 350°F (175°C); bake until golden brown and bubbling, about 30 to 40 minutes more. When there are about 10 minutes of bake time left, open the oven, pull the pie out, and quickly and evenly sprinkle the top of the pie with sugar.
8. Let the pie cool before serving so the filling can set up.

VARIATION

· · · · ·

MULBERRY PIE Substitute fresh picked mulberries for blackberries. The slender berries are very tender and their fragile stems almost disappear during the bake.

BLACKCAP PIE Substitute fresh picked blackcap berries (also known as black raspberries) for blackberries. I don't get blackcaps often and when I do, I stop everything and make a pie.

Blueberry Pie

My favorite blueberries are the ones that ripen later in the summer season; they are smaller and darker and pack a wallop of intense flavor. Blueberries that are larger and lighter may look pretty, but might not be as flavorful. Be sure to ask for a taste at the farmers' market or the produce section in your grocery to judge for yourself.

MAKES ONE 9-INCH DEEP-DISH PIE

INGREDIENTS
. . . . .

5–6 cups (790 grams), about 1¾ pounds, blueberries, fresh or unthawed frozen

¾ cup (150 grams) sugar

A small grating of freshly ground nutmeg

⅓ teaspoon (2 grams) salt

1 teaspoon (5 grams) freshly squeezed lemon juice

1 tablespoon (15 grams) orange liqueur, or zest of one small organic orange (optional)

⅓ cup (48 grams) flour

2 tablespoons (24 grams) quick-cooking tapioca

1 recipe double-crust pie dough

½ tablespoon (7 grams) butter

1 tablespoon (12 grams) sugar, for sprinkling on top of the pie

EGG WASH

1 egg white plus 1 tablespoon (15 grams) water, fork beaten

CONTINUED

PROCEDURE

· · · · ·

1. Preheat the oven to 425°F (220°C).

2. Put the blueberries, sugar, nutmeg, salt, lemon juice, optional orange liqueur or citrus zest, flour, and quick-cooking tapioca in a big bowl, and mix lightly until the fruit is coated.

3. Roll out the bottom dough and place it in your pie pan.

4. Add the blueberry filling and dot it with little pieces of butter.

5. Roll out remaining dough, lay it over the fruit, trim, crimp, and cut 5 to 6 vents on top, or cut strips and weave a lattice top (see Vents, Appliqués, Crimps, Flutes, Lattice, pages 51–56).

6. Brush the crust with some egg white wash.

7. Bake for 20 minutes at 425°F (220°C). Reduce the heat to 350°F (175°C) and bake for 35 to 40 minutes more. When there are 10 to 15 minutes of bake time left, open the oven, pull the pie out, and quickly and evenly sprinkle the top of the pie with sugar. Close the oven and continue baking for another 10 to 15 minutes. Look for the steady bubbling of the fruit filling coming through the vents or latticework to make sure the filling is fully cooked.

8. Cool the pie before serving so the fruit filling can set up.

Blueberry Crumble Pie

Crumble toppings sometimes brown too much before the filling is done, so wait for the last twenty minutes of the bake to sprinkle this oat crumble evenly over the top. If you have one disc of dough on hand, and a bag of pre-made topping in the freezer, this pie is a snap to make.

MAKES ONE 9-INCH DEEP-DISH PIE

INGREDIENTS
· · · · ·

1 recipe Crumble Topping (see page 95)

5–6 cups (790 grams), about 1¾ pounds, blueberries, fresh or unthawed frozen

¾ cup (150 grams) sugar

A small grating of freshly ground nutmeg

⅓ teaspoon (2 grams) salt

1 teaspoon (6 grams) freshly squeezed lemon juice

1 tablespoon (15 grams) Cointreau or other orange liqueur, or zest of one small organic orange (optional)

½ cup (48 grams) flour

1 tablespoon (12 grams) quick-cooking tapioca

1 recipe single-crust pie dough

CONTINUED

PROCEDURE

· · · · ·

1. Prepare Crumble Topping and chill in the freezer for at least 15 minutes while you make the filling.

2. Preheat the oven to 425°F (220°C).

3. Put the blueberries, sugar, nutmeg, salt, lemon juice, optional orange liqueur or citrus zest, flour, and quick-cooking tapioca in a big bowl, and mix lightly until the fruit is well coated.

4. Roll out the bottom dough and place it in your pie pan. Trim excess dough from the edges and crimp.

5. Add the blueberry filling.

6. Bake for 20 minutes at 425°F (220°C). Reduce the heat to 350°F (175°C) and, after 20 minutes, sprinkle the frozen crumble topping over the top of the filling evenly. Continue to bake for 20 more minutes.

7. Look for the steady bubbling of the fruit filling coming through the crumble topping to make sure the filling is fully cooked.

8. Cool the pie before serving so the fruit filling can set up.

Raspberry Pie

When I think of sweet red raspberries I can't help but call to mind my friend Melissa, who grows a great profusion of them on her little farm facing the Olympic Mountains. The little red berries are shy and sweet, like her.

MAKES ONE 9-INCH DEEP-DISH PIE

INGREDIENTS
. . . . .

6 cups (752 grams), about 1⅔ pounds, raspberries, fresh or unthawed frozen; enough to fill the pie pan ½ inch below the rim

¾ cup (150 grams) sugar

A small grating of freshly ground nutmeg

⅓ teaspoon (2 grams) salt

¼ cup (36 grams) flour

2 teaspoons (8 grams) quick-cooking tapioca

1 tablespoon (15 grams) Cointreau or other orange liqueur (optional)

1 recipe double-crust pie dough

½ tablespoon (7 grams) butter

1–2 teaspoons (4–8 grams) sugar, for sprinkling on top of pie

EGG WASH

1 egg white plus 1 tablespoon (15 grams) water, fork beaten

PROCEDURE

· · · · ·

1. Preheat the oven to 425°F (220°C).

2. Place the raspberries, sugar, nutmeg, salt, flour, tapioca, and Cointreau in a medium bowl and mix lightly to coat all the fruit.

3. Roll out the bottom dough and place it in your pie pan.

4. Add the raspberry filling and dot it with little pieces of butter.

5. Roll out the remaining dough, lay it over the fruit, and cut 5 to 6 vents on top, or cut strips and make a lattice top. Trim excess dough from the edges and crimp (see Vents, Appliqués, Crimps, Flutes, Lattice, pages 51–56).

6. Lightly brush some of the egg white wash over the entire pie, including the edges.

7. Bake for 20 minutes at 425°F (220°C). Reduce the heat to 350°F (175°C) and bake for 35 to 40 minutes more. When there are about 10 minutes of bake time left, open the oven, pull the pie out, and quickly and evenly sprinkle the top of the pie with sugar. Close the oven and continue to bake. Look for the steady bubbling of the fruit filling through the vents or latticework to make sure the filling is fully cooked.

8. Let the pie cool before serving so the filling can set up.

· · · · · · · · · · · · · · · · · · NOTE · · · · · · · · · · · · · · · · · ·

Serve with a dollop of whipped cream or a scoop of vanilla ice cream.

· ·

Raspberry Salmonberry Pie

How many folks can say that they have their own forager? Not too many, I would wager. But I'm lucky to have a good one in my neck of the woods. When my friend Cathy was visiting, I made a pie with baskets of just-picked salmonberries he delivered right to my cottage door. Cathy called the red, orange, and yellow berries "a party in a bowl." Salmonberries are a safe wild berry but not as sweet as most cultivated berries we buy at the store. They grow west of the Cascade Mountains from Alaska to California. I add a few ripe raspberries to sweeten the filling up a bit more. If you can't get them, throw in another berry like blackberries.

MAKES ONE 9-INCH DEEP-DISH PIE

INGREDIENTS

· · · · ·

3 cups (340 grams), about ¾ pound, ripe salmonberries

3 cups (340 grams), about ¾ pound, ripe raspberries

¾ cup (150 grams) sugar, adjust as needed for the tartness of the berries and the size of your pie pan

1–2 gratings freshly ground nutmeg, a pinch

1 teaspoon (5 grams) freshly squeezed lemon juice

⅓ teaspoon (2 grams) salt

½ cup (73 grams) flour, or ¼ cup (36 grams) quick-cooking tapioca

1 recipe double-crust pie dough

1 knob butter, the size of a small walnut, for dotting the top of the filling

1 tablespoon (12 grams) sugar, for sprinkling on top of the pie

EGG WASH

1 egg white plus 1 tablespoon (15 grams) water, fork beaten

PROCEDURE
· · · · ·

1. Preheat the oven to 425°F (220°C).

2. Put the berries, sugar, nutmeg, lemon juice, salt, and flour or tapioca into a bowl and mix gently until combined. Don't overmix so you can keep the shape of the berries, although smushing a few with the back side of a wooden spoon is fine, and makes a nice texture.

3. Roll out the bottom dough and place it in your pie pan.

4. Pour the filling into a pie pan and dot with butter.

5. Roll out the remaining dough, lay it over the fruit, and cut 5 to 6 vents on top, or cut strips and make a lattice top. Trim excess dough and crimp edges of pie (see Vents, Appliqués, Crimps, Flutes, Lattice, pages 51–56).

6. Paint the dough with egg white wash.

7. Bake at 425°F (220°C) for 20 minutes. Reduce the heat to 375°F (190°C) and bake for 35 minutes more.

8. When there are 10 to 15 minutes of bake time left, open the oven, pull the pie out, and quickly and evenly sprinkle the top of the pie with sugar. Close the oven and continue baking until you see steady bubbling in the filling coming through the vents or lattice.

9. Cool the pie before serving so the fruit filling can set up.

· · · · · · · · · · · · · · · · · · NOTES · · · · · · · · · · · · · · · · · ·

Fill your pie pan ½ inch below the rim to avoid a spillover of fruit filling.

If it needs more spicing or sweetening, the time to do it is before you turn it into the bottom crust. Feel free to add ½ teaspoon cinnamon, or any other seasoning you like.

· ·

Triple Berry Pie

If one berry is good, two berries are better, and when blackberries, blueberries, and raspberries are all ripe, three are best of all. Use equal parts of the berries in this filling plus a few extra for the obligatory tasting. Remember to fill to one-half inch below the rim of the pie pan so it won't bubble over during the bake.

MAKES ONE 9-INCH DEEP-DISH PIE

INGREDIENTS

· · · · ·

6 cups (680–900 grams), about 1½–2 pounds, equal parts blackberries, blueberries, raspberries, fresh picked or unthawed frozen

¾ cup (150 grams) sugar

A very small grating or pinch of fresh nutmeg

1 teaspoon (5 grams) freshly squeezed lemon juice and a few gratings of lemon zest

⅛ teaspoon (2 grams) salt

⅓ cup (48 grams) flour

1 teaspoon (4 grams) quick-cooking tapioca

1 recipe double-crust pie dough

1 knob butter, the size of a small walnut, cut into small pieces for dotting the top of the filling

1–2 teaspoons (4–8 grams) sugar, for sprinkling on top of the pie

EGG WASH

1 egg white plus 1 tablespoon (15 grams) water, fork beaten

PROCEDURE

· · · · ·

1. Preheat the oven to 425°F (220°C).

2. Put the berries, sugar, nutmeg, lemon juice, zest, salt, flour, and tapioca into a bowl and mix. Using a wooden spoon, mash gently to make a textured filling. Pour the mixture into the chilled crust, dot with butter, and set aside.

3. Roll out the bottom dough and place it in a pie plate or pan.

4. Roll out the remaining dough, lay it over the fruit, and cut 5 to 6 vents on top, or arrange strips over pie in a lattice. Trim excess dough and finish the edges of pie with a fork crimp, flutes or scallops (see Vents, Appliqués, Crimps, Flutes, Lattice, pages 51–56).

5. Brush the dough with the egg white mixture.

6. Bake at 425°F (220°C) on the middle rack of the oven until the crust is golden brown, about 15 to 20 minutes. Reduce the heat to 350°F (175°C) and bake until golden brown and bubbling, about 30 to 40 minutes more. When there are about 10 minutes of bake time left, open the oven, pull the pie out, and quickly and evenly sprinkle the top of the pie with sugar. Continue to bake for remaining time.

7. Cool the pie before serving so the fruit filling can set up.

· · · · · · · · · · · · · · · · · **PIE BASKETS** · · · · · · · · · · · · · · · · ·

Some have lids, some not; one is decorated with small hand-painted strawberries, another has a wooden tray stained with the juice of berries. These treasures seem to show up at antique and estate sales, and I am always on the lookout to add more to my collection. I spied a lovely lidded one at a sale, shyly and patiently peering out from underneath rolling pins, pancake turners, and other kitchen utensils displayed within it. "This is mine," I said to the vendor, who seemed delighted. As I was placing the well-worn handles over my arm, she asked me, "What will you do with it?" "Use it to carry pies, of course!"

· ·

Forest Berry Pie

When Robin, my son's sweetheart, was a young girl growing up on Whidbey Island, she and her brothers, David and Peter, roamed the forest trails foraging for ripe wild huckleberries, blackberries, boysenberries, thimbleberries, and salmonberries for pie. Every time the mix was different, but always delicious. Make sure you can safely identify berries before you eat them.

MAKES ONE 9-INCH DEEP-DISH PIE

INGREDIENTS
· · · · ·

6 cups (918 grams), about 2 pounds, any combination of freshly picked huckleberries, blackberries, boysenberries, thimbleberries, and salmonberries

¾–1 cup (150–200 grams) sugar, depending on the tartness of the berries

A small grating of freshly ground nutmeg

1 teaspoon (5 grams) freshly squeezed lemon juice and a few gratings of lemon zest

½ teaspoon (3 grams) salt

⅓ cup (48 grams) flour

½–1 tablespoon (6–12 grams) quick-cooking tapioca, if fruit is especially juicy

1 recipe double-crust pie dough

1 tablespoon (14 grams) cold butter, cut into small pieces

1–2 teaspoons (4–8 grams) sugar, for sprinkling on top of the pie

EGG WASH

1 egg white plus 1 tablespoon (15 grams) water, fork beaten

PROCEDURE

· · · · ·

1. Preheat the oven to 425°F (220°C).

2. Put the berries, sugar, nutmeg, lemon juice, zest, salt, flour, and tapioca into a bowl and mix. Using the back of a wooden spoon, mash gently to make a textured filling.

3. Roll out the bottom dough and place it in a pie pan. Cover it with plastic wrap and chill for 10 to 15 minutes while you make the filling.

4. Pour the filling into the chilled crust, dot with butter, and set aside.

5. Roll out the remaining dough, lay it over the fruit, and cut 5 to 6 vents on top, or arrange strips over the pie in a lattice. Trim excess dough and finish the edges of the pie with a fork crimp, flutes or scallops (see Vents, Appliqués, Crimps, Flutes, Lattice, pages 51–56).

6. Brush the dough with egg white mixture.

7. Bake for 20 minutes at 425°F (220°C). Reduce the heat to 350°F (175°C) and bake for 30 minutes more. When there are about 10 minutes of bake time left, open the oven, pull the pie out, and quickly and evenly sprinkle the top of the pie with sugar. Close the oven and continue baking for another 10 minutes, or until you see steady bubbling in the filling coming through the vents or lattice.

8. Cool the pie before serving so the fruit filling can set up.

Huckleberry Pie

Huckleberries are a highly anticipated summer treat in the Northwest, and I see them popping up in grocery store freezer sections, too. If you live in an area like Montana or Washington and spy fresh huckleberries at a farmers' market, buy enough to make fresh pies and freeze the rest for special desserts throughout the year.

MAKES ONE 9-INCH DEEP-DISH PIE

INGREDIENTS
· · · · ·

5–6 cups (790 grams), about 1¾ pounds, black or red huckleberries, fresh or unthawed frozen

¾ cup (150 grams) sugar

A small grating of freshly ground nutmeg

⅓ teaspoon (2 grams) salt

1 teaspoon (5 grams) freshly squeezed lemon juice

1 tablespoon (15 grams) orange liqueur, or zest of one small organic orange (optional)

⅓ cup (48 grams) flour

2 tablespoons (24 grams) quick-cooking tapioca

1 recipe double-crust pie dough

½ tablespoon (7 grams) butter

2 teaspoons (8 grams) sugar for sprinkling on top of the pie

EGG WASH

1 egg white plus 1 tablespoon (15 grams) water, fork beaten

PROCEDURE

· · · · ·

1. Preheat the oven to 425°F (220°C).

2. Put the huckleberries, sugar, nutmeg, salt, lemon juice, optional orange liqueur or citrus zest, flour, and quick-cooking tapioca in a big bowl, and mix lightly until the fruit is coated.

3. Roll out the bottom dough and place it in your pie pan.

4. Add the huckleberry filling and dot with little pieces of butter.

5. Roll out the remaining dough, lay it over the fruit, trim, crimp, and cut 5 to 6 vents on top, or cut strips and weave a lattice top (see Vents, Appliqués, Crimps, Flutes, Lattice, pages 51–56).

6. Brush the crust with some egg white wash.

7. Bake for 20 minutes. Reduce the heat to 350°F (175°C) and, after about 45 minutes total time, open the oven and quickly sprinkle the top of the pie with sugar. Close the oven and continue baking for another 10 to 15 minutes, or until you see steady bubbling in the filling coming through the vents or lattice. If the top of the pie looks like it is browning too quickly, cover the top of the pie with a piece of foil, turned shiny side down, with a vent torn in the middle.

8. Cool the pie before serving so the fruit filling can set up.

Marionberry Pie

Marionberries are a cultivated berry first developed in Marion County, Oregon in 1956. These berries have an intense blackberry flavor that is both tart and sweet, and have even been called the cabernet or queen of blackberries. If you can't find them fresh, unthawed frozen berries will make a fine pie.

MAKES ONE 9-INCH DEEP-DISH PIE

INGREDIENTS
· · · · ·

6 cups (680–900 grams), about 1½–2 pounds marionberries, fresh picked or unthawed frozen

¾ cup (150 grams) sugar

A small grating or pinch of fresh nutmeg

1 teaspoon (5 grams) freshly squeezed lemon juice

⅓ teaspoon (2 grams) salt

⅓ cup (48 grams) flour

1 recipe double-crust pie dough

1 tablespoon (14 grams) butter, cut into small pieces

1–2 teaspoons (4–8 grams) sugar, for sprinkling on top of the pie

EGG WASH

1 egg white plus 1 tablespoon (15 grams) water, fork beaten

PROCEDURE
· · · · ·

1. Preheat the oven to 425°F (220°C).

2. Put the marionberries, sugar, nutmeg lemon juice, salt, and flour into a bowl and mix. If using fresh berries, mix lightly.

3. Roll out the bottom dough and place it in a chilled pie plate or pan.

4. Pour the mixture into the dough, dot with butter, and set aside.

5. Roll out the remaining dough, lay it over the fruit, and cut 5 to 6 vents on top, or arrange strips over pie in a lattice. Trim excess dough and finish the edges of pie with a fork crimp, flutes, or scallops (see Vents, Appliqués, Crimps, Flutes, Lattice, pages 51–56).

6. Brush the dough with egg white mixture.

7. Bake for 20 minutes at 425°F (220°C). Reduce the heat to 350°F (175°C) and bake for 30 minutes more.

8. When there are about 10 minutes of bake time left, open the oven, pull the pie out, and quickly and evenly sprinkle the top of the pie with sugar. Close the oven and continue baking for another 10 minutes, or until you see steady bubbling in the filling coming through the vents or lattice.

9. Cool the pie before serving so the fruit filling can set up.

Red Currant Pie

I occasionally see red currants at my farm store during the summer, and if you have a bush of your own, pick the clusters when they are satiny and bright red to make this old-fashioned pie. Ripe currants have a sweet, tart, and some say slightly sour flavor. Add orange juice, zest, or liqueur for a unique pie to share at a potluck.

MAKES ONE 9-INCH SHALLOW PIE

INGREDIENTS
. . . . .

4 cups (612 grams) ripe red currants

1 cup (200 grams) sugar

⅓ cup plus 1 tablespoon (48 grams) cornstarch

A small grating of freshly ground nutmeg

¼ teaspoon (a pinch) salt

1 recipe double-crust pie dough

1 tablespoon (14 grams) butter

2 teaspoons (8 grams) sugar, for sprinkling on top of the pie

EGG WASH

1 egg white plus 1 tablespoon (15 grams) water, fork beaten

PROCEDURE

· · · · ·

1. Preheat the oven to 425°F (220°C).

2. Put the currants, sugar, cornstarch, nutmeg, and salt in a medium bowl. Mix well and set it aside.

3. Roll out the bottom dough and place it in your pie pan.

4. Add the currant filling and dot with butter, cut into little pieces.

5. Roll out the remaining dough, lay it over the fruit, and cut 5 to 6 vents on top, or cut strips and make a lattice top. Trim excess dough and finish the edges as you like (see Vents, Appliqués, Crimps, Flutes, Lattice, pages 51–56).

6. Brush the crust with egg white wash.

7. Bake for 20 minutes. Reduce the heat to 350°F (175°C) and bake for 35 to 40 minutes more.

8. When there are about 10 minutes of bake time left, open the oven, pull the pie out, and quickly and evenly sprinkle the top of the pie with sugar.

9. Look for the steady bubbling of the fruit filling through the vents or latticework to make sure the filling is fully cooked.

10. Let the pie cool before serving so the filling can set up.

· NOTES ·

If you have gooseberries, mix equally with the currants.
Black currants may be used in place of red currants, but
add a bit more sugar to taste.

· ·

Gooseberry Pie

I absolutely love a good old-fashioned gooseberry pie. The fruit has been used in Britain as far back as the thirteenth century, and for pies in the United States, since pioneer days. Happily, I am starting to see them come back onto the commercial market, albeit in small quantities. The gooseberry season in the summertime is short, so I buy as many as I can fit into my refrigerator when I spy them. They are not so fragile, and can hold for a week, and sometimes more. Gooseberries are tart, so adjust for sweetness by tasting the filling and adding more sugar as you go. You can always add sugar and spice, but it's much harder to take it out. I use red, or the more common green, gooseberries in this pie, and a combination of both is quite wonderful. Check Frieda's (friedas.com) to find a store with gooseberries in your area.

MAKES ONE 9-INCH DEEP-DISH PIE

INGREDIENTS
· · · · ·

6 cups (680–900 grams), about 1½–2 pounds, red or green gooseberries, or a combination of the two (adjust amount for the size of your pan)

1 cup (200 grams) sugar—add more to taste

A small grating of freshly ground nutmeg

⅓ teaspoon (2 grams) salt

½ teaspoon (3 grams) freshly squeezed lemon juice

2½ tablespoons (30 grams) quick-cooking tapioca

2 tablespoons (16 grams) flour

1 recipe double-crust pie dough

1 knob butter, about the size of a small walnut

1–2 teaspoons (4–8 grams) sugar

EGG WASH

1 egg white plus 1 tablespoon (15 grams) water, fork beaten

PROCEDURE

· · · · ·

1. Preheat the oven to 425°F (220°C).

2. Put gooseberries, sugar, nutmeg, salt, lemon juice, tapioca, and flour in a medium bowl and mix lightly until the berries are coated with all the other ingredients.

3. Roll out the bottom dough and place it in your pie pan.

4. Add the fruit filling. Take the knob of butter, break it into little pieces with your fingers, and dot the top of the filling. It's okay if you forget to dot with butter; a lot of times I do, too.

5. Roll out the remaining dough, lay it over the fruit, and cut 5 to 6 vents on top, or cut strips and make a lattice top. Trim excess dough and finish the edges however you like (see Vents, Appliqués, Crimps, Flutes, Lattice, pages 51–56).

6. Brush the dough with egg white wash.

7. Bake for 15 minutes. Reduce the heat to 375°F (190°C) and bake for 35 minutes more. When there are about 10 minutes of bake time left, open the oven, pull the pie out, and quickly and evenly sprinkle the top of the pie with sugar. Bake until it's golden brown and there is some steady bubbling and steam coming through the vents.

8. Cool the pie before serving so the fruit filling can set up.

· · · · · · · · · · · · · · · SUGAR · · · · · · · · · · · · · · ·

Use a mesh tea strainer—one of the little ones with a handle like a spoon—for a very even sprinkle of sugar on top of the pie.

· ·

Concord Grape Pie

If you like grape juice, this is just the pie for you. The filling takes a bit more preparation because the grapes need to be peeled. I know that this sounds like a very laborious process, but it's much easier than pitting cherries. All you have to do is hold a grape in your fingers opposite the stem end and squeeze until the grape pops out. This rich pie can be made open-face or with a full top crust. Chop the skins up before pouring the hot pulp over them or keep them whole. I like the look and texture both ways.

MAKES ONE 9-INCH SHALLOW PIE

INGREDIENTS
· · · · ·

6 cups (680–900 grams), about 1½–2 pounds, Concord grapes, washed

¾ cup (150 grams) sugar

1 teaspoon (5 grams) freshly squeezed lemon juice

1 tablespoon (15 grams) Cointreau or other orange liqueur

A small grating of freshly ground nutmeg (optional)

⅛ teaspoon (a small pinch) salt

¼ cup plus 1 tablespoon (40 grams) flour

1 recipe double-crust pie dough or ½ recipe if making an open-face pie

1 knob butter, about the size of a small walnut

1–2 teaspoons (4–8 grams) sugar for sprinkling on top of the pie, if you're making it with an upper crust

EGG WASH IF MAKING WITH AN UPPER CRUST

1 egg white plus 1 tablespoon (15 grams) water, fork beaten

CONTINUED

PROCEDURE

· · · · ·

1. Peel the grapes and place them in bowl. To peel the grapes, hold one in your fingers opposite the stem end and then squeeze it out of its skin into a bowl. Place the skins in a separate small bowl and set aside.

2. Place the skinless grapes in a heavy saucepan over high heat, and let them boil for about 5 minutes. Watch as they spit many of their seeds out.

3. Remove the grapes from the heat and spoon out as many of the seeds as possible before putting the hot grapes and their juice into a food mill. Process the grapes into a smooth pulp.

4. Pour the hot grape pulp over chopped or whole grape skins, stir, cover, and let it sit overnight in the fridge.

5. When you're ready to assemble, preheat the oven to 450°F (230°C).

6. Add the sugar, lemon juice, Cointreau, nutmeg, salt, and flour to the grape pulp mixture, and mix.

7. Roll out the pie dough and place it in a pan.

8. Pour in the grape pulp mixture and dot with butter.

9. If you would like an upper crust on the pie, roll out the second dough and cover the fruit, then seal, trim, and crimp the edges (see Vents, Appliqués, Crimps, Flutes, Lattice, pages 51–56).

10. Brush the dough with egg white wash.

11. Bake at 450°F (230°C) for 15 minutes and then turn the heat down to 350°F (175°C) and continue to bake for another 25 minutes. When there are about 10 minutes of bake time left, open the oven, pull the pie out, and quickly and evenly sprinkle the top of the pie with sugar.

12. Remove the pie from the oven and let it cool. This pie can be served warm or cold.

Clean the Oven Pie

This is a pie we have all made . . . at least once.

MAKES ONE PIE

INGREDIENTS
. . . . .

1 recipe fruit filling

1 recipe double- or single-crust pie dough

PROCEDURE
. . . . .

1. Preheat the oven to 425°F (220°C). Make your favorite pie filling with fresh or unthawed frozen fruit (berries, pie cherries, rhubarb, etc.)—the juicier the better.
2. Mound it really high.
3. Cover it with a top crust and cut vents or make a lattice crust (see Vents, Appliqués, Crimps, Flutes, Lattice, pages 51–56).
4. Bake it in the oven.
5. You will know when it is nearly done when you start to smell burning filling.
6. Open the oven to release smoke.
7. Fan the smoke away from the smoke alarm that is now going off. Open windows at this time, too.
8. Remove the pie from the oven when it has bubbled over enough.
9. While the pie cools, clean your oven.

CHAPTER FIVE

Sweet as a Peach

(and Other Stone Fruits)

Farmer Al is a wizard of flavor and I think his

peaches might be the best in the world. At Frog Hollow, his farm in Brentwood, California, he knows how to coax every possible bit of sweetness from the trees in his orchards straight into the legendary fruit he grows in them. We're talking the kind of peach you better lean way over to eat, because when you take a bite, incredibly sweet juice will run down your chin and over your fingers while you try to slurp it back into your mouth so as not to miss one single drop. I met Al when he was visiting Seattle in 2000 and tasted one of his peaches soon after. I've heard it said that eating a perfect peach might possibly change one's life. I guess it did for me, because that first bite of peach was like tasting the sun. I realized that the flavor of every peach I had eaten before then was inadequate. Even though Frog Hollow peaches are far afield from the 100-mile radius I try to eat within, having his Cal Reds for pies and out-of-hand eating in the summertime is an exception I have absolutely no qualms about making.

Farmer Al and his wife, Becky, who creates the fruit-filled pastries they also sell, are raising two beautiful daughters, Maddie and Millie, already on track to become the next generation of Frog Hollow peach farmers. How lucky I was when Becky opened up her farm kitchen during harvest season for a pie-making workshop. Our goal was to make and bake perfect peach pies with fruit we would harvest right from the trees. On a warm Sunday afternoon, four pie makers and I piled onto a farm cart, and Farmer Al drove us through rows and rows of his trees, proudly pointing out apricot, nectarine, and plum. Stopping between two rows of peach trees that had that day's very best fruit, we got out and watched as Farmer Al found a perfectly ripe specimen on a branch and showed it to us. "There should be no green surrounding the stem. If there is, it's not ready to pick. When the green is replaced by gold, and can be pulled off the branch easily—then is it ready for harvest," he said, and we passed it around to see for ourselves. We learned that if you hold two peaches of similar size, one in each hand, always to choose the heaviest, as it has more sugar and will taste sweeter. Farmer Al picked a few more, and, with his knife, cut slices dripping with juice for us to try. Our first bites were followed by involuntary moans. These peaches were perfect.

Having now tasted the best, we set out to find our own. We looked for gold near the stem to complement the beautiful reddish blush on the skin. We evaluated their weight, and added the heaviest to our pie plates. When full, we climbed back aboard the farm cart, and Farmer Al drove us back through the orchard to Becky's kitchen where we made picture-perfect pies with the sweetest peaches any of us had ever tasted. Mission accomplished.

Best Peach Pie in the World

(The Long Wordy Version)

Of all the pies I make, peach pie is my absolute favorite in the whole world. I don't limit it to just dessert, and I hope you won't either. Have it for breakfast, for lunch, for dinner, for a midnight snack, and then do it all over again. With a lattice-top crust, a full top with vents, or a free-form crostata, a sweet, ripe peach pie is a thing of beauty.

What you need right now are two pounds of pie-worthy peaches—ones that are sweet but still have a tiny bit of acid in them, causing you to burst into song and do a little happy dance when you take a bite. Maybe you are lucky enough to have peaches like these growing right in your own yard, and if you do, let me tell you how I envy you. The rest of us will be checking our grocery stores, farmers' markets, and farm stands in hopes of striking it rich. Ask the grower or your greengrocer for a taste, and if it knocks your socks off, then buy a case or two . . . maybe even three. After all, peaches like these only come once a year.

I use freestone peaches because the pits come out easily. Yes, you can use cling peaches, but do yourself a favor and get a freestone variety because it will be easier in the prep department. I give the fruit a little rinse but don't bother to peel them. The skins will fade into the background in the filling when baked. Slice each peach in half and take out the pit. Cut each peach half in thirds, and, depending on the size of the slices, cut the thirds into three or four chunks after that. Put the chunks into the pie pan until the height averages about one-half inch below the rim. Inevitably some chunks will be a bit higher. Don't worry about being too exact, but don't mound this pie too high or the peach juice will be boiling over onto the oven floor when it bakes, and you'll be cleaning it up later. If you add too much fruit, you can reduce the amount by sampling and snacking on them as you add the rest of the ingredients to the filling. When it looks right, you'll know. Transfer the peaches from the pie pan into a mixing bowl, then rinse and dry the pan and set it underneath the bowl—this will give you more counter space, always hard to come by in my tiny kitchen.

You've tasted the peaches already, haven't you? If you haven't, stop right now and take a bite. This will give you an idea of how much sweetener to add. Start with one-quarter to one-half cup of sugar. "So little?" you say. If there's a lot of sweet flavor in your peaches, you may not have to add any sugar at all. You can taste the results in a minute or two, but for now let's keep going.

Add a pinch of salt, and then a fresh grating of nutmeg—just enough so you can smell its aroma when you get your nose down close to the fruit in the bowl. If you like cinnamon, or another spice like ginger, you can put that in now, too. I like this filling when I can still taste the peaches, so nutmeg does it for me, but this is your pie, so add what you want.

Farmers talk about fruit's acid-sweet balance. When you get a peach that has the balance just right, there is a bright quality in addition to the sweetness, but I still like to add a little squeeze of lemon. Too much can be overwhelming, so go slow here because you can't take it away if you put in too much. Adjust the size of the squeeze of lemon to how bright you want your filling to taste. Start with a small squeeze, and add another small squeeze after tasting the filling if you feel it needs it. Then add some Cointreau. Just tip the bottle and say "Whoops!" as it goes in. I add a small amount of this orange liqueur to pies. In fact, I have won contests using it in pie fillings—one judge even wrote, "Yum. Yum. Yum. Yum" in his scorecard remarks section, wondering just what that secret ingredient was. I didn't tell him, but I'm sharing my secret with you.

Peaches are juicy, so we're going to use two thickeners. Start with a handful of quick-cooking tapioca, which I think is a pie maker's best friend, and then follow that with some flour (either all-purpose or Gluten-Free Flour Mix on page 79). Lightly but thoroughly mix and then take a taste. Adjust the seasoning and sweetener to your own taste. When you can't stop taking bites, set the filling aside while you roll out your dough and place it in the pie pan. When the bottom crust is settled into the pan, fold the filling into it and move right on to rolling out the top crust. You might make a pretty lattice top or a cut a few carefully placed vents on a full top (see Vents, Appliqués, Crimps, Flutes, Lattice, on pages 51–56). Both are fine. Then let your pie chill in the fridge while you place a baking sheet in the middle of the oven, preheat to 425°F (220°C), and tidy up the kitchen.

Paint the top of the pie with a little egg white mixed with water and then place it in the oven on the heated baking sheet. After twenty minutes, turn the oven down to 375°F (190°C) and continue baking for another twenty-five minutes. Next, open the oven up, pull the pie out, and sprinkle a little sugar on top. Slide the pie back inside to bake some more until the top looks golden-brown and the fruit filling is bubbling up through the vents. You've got to see those steady bubbles to gauge whether the tapioca has done its work. If the pie has been in there for nearly one hour and you're still not seeing the bubbles, cover the top of the pie loosely with a sheet of aluminum foil (shiny side down, with a little vent torn in the middle), crank the oven up to 445°F (230°C), and let it bake for another six minutes. Why six? I don't know, other than that's what works in my oven.

When you see bubbles dancing between the lattice strips and through the vents, pull the pie out and let it cool so the filling can set up. While it cools, you will need to make an important decision: whether to share with your neighbors, or not. If it's the former, than open your window and sing out "Peach pie!" Your neighbors will be there shortly and that just-baked pie might quickly disappear. If it's the latter, get out your fork and dig right in.

My Favorite Peach Pie
(The Short Tidy Version)

Peach pie is one of the absolute best ways to make friends of your neighbors. If they don't love you after eating this pie, then I believe there just might be a serious question as to their character to begin with. I could tell you the story of the man who moved next door to Pie Cottage and told me he didn't like pie when I brought him one as a welcome gift. I should have known right then and there that he was not going to stick around for long. But that's a story for another day. This pie is very juicy, so be sure to add extra thickener to the filling.

MAKES ONE 9-INCH DEEP-DISH PIE

INGREDIENTS
· · · · ·

6 cups (680–900 grams), about 1½–2 pounds, sweet, ripe, free-stone peaches, halved, pitted, sliced and chopped

¼–½ cup (50–100 grams) sugar; adjust for the sweetness of the fruit

A small pinch of fresh ground nutmeg, enough that you can smell it when you lean down close to the bowl

½ teaspoon (3 grams) freshly squeezed lemon juice

2–3 teaspoons (10–15 grams) Cointreau or other orange liqueur (optional)

⅓ teaspoon (2 grams) salt

¼ cup (36 grams) flour

2 tablespoons (24 grams) quick-cooking tapioca

1 recipe double-crust pie dough

½ tablespoon (7 grams) butter

1–2 teaspoons (4–8 grams) sugar, for sprinkling on top of the pie

EGG WASH

1 egg white plus 1 tablespoon (15 grams) water, fork beaten

PROCEDURE

· · · · ·

1. Preheat the oven to 425°F (220°C).

2. Place the peaches, sugar, nutmeg, lemon juice, Cointreau, salt, flour, and quick-cooking tapioca in a big bowl. Mix lightly until the fruit is coated.

3. Roll out the bottom dough and place it in a pie pan.

4. Spoon in the fruit filling and dot with butter cut into little pieces with your fingers.

5. Roll out the remaining dough, lay it over the fruit, and cut 5 to 6 vents on top, or cut strips and make a lattice top. Trim excess dough from the edges and crimp (see Vents, Appliqués, Crimps, Flutes, Lattice, pages 51–56).

6. Lightly brush some of the egg white wash over the entire pie, including the edges.

7. Bake for 20 minutes at 425°F (220°C). Reduce the heat to 375°F (190°C) and bake for 40 to 45 minutes more. When there are 10 to 15 minutes of bake time left, open the oven, pull the pie out, and quickly and evenly sprinkle the top of the pie with sugar. Close the oven and continue baking for another 10 to 15 minutes, or until you see steady bubbling in the filling coming through the vents or lattice.

8. Remove the pie from the oven and cool completely before serving so the filling can set up, although warm peach pie is delicious.

· · · · · · · · · · · · · · · · · · **NOTE** · · · · · · · · · · · · · · · · · ·

This recipe uses the preheat first, no time to chill the pie method (see page 117), but use what works best for you depending on time and temperature.

· ·

Peach Berry Pie

Raspberry-peach, blackberry-peach, blueberry-peach, or a combination of all three makes a fabulous pie. Because berries and peaches ripen at just about the same time, it's easy to make this one with fresh fruit.

MAKES ONE 9-INCH DEEP-DISH PIE

INGREDIENTS

. . . . .

4 cups (450 grams), about 1 pound, peaches, sliced

2 cups (226 grams), about ½ pound, raspberries, blackberries, or blueberries, or a combination

¾ cup (150 grams) sugar

A small grating of freshly ground nutmeg

⅓ teaspoon (2 grams) salt

¼ cup (36 grams) flour

1½ tablespoons (18 grams) quick-cooking tapioca

1 recipe double-crust pie dough

½ tablespoon (7 grams) butter

1–2 teaspoons (4–8 grams) sugar, for sprinkling on top of the pie

EGG WASH

1 egg white plus 1 tablespoon (15 grams) water, fork beaten

PROCEDURE

· · · · ·

1. Preheat the oven to 425°F (220°C).
2. Place the peaches, berries, sugar, nutmeg, salt, flour, and tapioca in a medium bowl and mix lightly to coat all the fruit.
3. Roll out the bottom dough and place it in your pie pan.
4. Add the berry-peach filling and dot with little pieces of butter.
5. Roll out the remaining dough, lay it over the fruit, and cut 5 to 6 vents on top, or cut strips and make a lattice top. Trim excess dough from the edges and crimp (see Vents, Appliqués, Crimps, Flutes, Lattice, pages 51–56).
6. Lightly brush some of the egg white wash over the entire pie, including the edges.
7. Bake for 20 minutes at 425°F (220°C). Reduce the heat to 350°F (175°C) and bake for 35 to 40 minutes more. When there are about 10 minutes of bake time left, open the oven, pull the pie out, and quickly and evenly sprinkle the top of the pie with sugar. Look for the steady bubbling of the fruit filling through the vents or lattice-work to make sure the filling is fully cooked.
8. Let the pie cool before serving so the filling can set up.

Blueberry Peach Pie

This pie combines two of my favorite fruits from two of my favorite farms: Blueberry Haven Farm on Washington's Olympic Peninsula and Frog Hollow Farm in California, where Farmer Al grows the sweetest peaches. I use his Cal Red peaches when I can get them, but any juicy peach, as long as it has great flavor, will do. I like to use late-season blueberries that are smaller, darker, and pack a wallop of blueberry flavor. Be sure to taste the fruit and adjust the sugar accordingly.

MAKES ONE 9-INCH DEEP-DISH PIE

INGREDIENTS

. . . . .

2 cups (250 grams), about 10 ounces, blueberries, fresh or unthawed frozen

4 cups (450 grams), about 1 pound, ripe peaches, halved, pitted, chopped, or sliced

½–1 cup (100–200 grams) granulated sugar, depending on sweetness of fruit

A small grating of freshly ground nutmeg

⅓ teaspoon (2 grams) salt

1 teaspoon (6 grams) freshly squeezed lemon juice

1 tablespoon (15 grams) Cointreau or other orange liqueur or zest of one orange (optional)

¼ cup (36 grams) flour

2 teaspoons (8 grams) quick-cooking tapioca

1 recipe double-crust pie dough

½ tablespoon (7 grams) butter

1–2 teaspoons (4–8 grams) sugar, for sprinkling on top of the pie

EGG WASH

1 egg white plus 1 tablespoon (15 grams) water, fork beaten

PROCEDURE

· · · · ·

1. Preheat the oven to 425°F (220°C).

2. Put the blueberries, peaches, sugar, nutmeg, salt, lemon juice, optional Cointreau or orange zest, flour, and quick-cooking tapioca in a big bowl, and mix lightly until the fruit is coated.

3. Roll out the bottom dough and place it in your pie pan.

4. Add the fruit filling and dot with little pieces of butter, if you remember.

5. Roll out the remaining dough, lay it over the fruit, and cut 5 to 6 vents on top, or cut strips and make a lattice top. Trim excess dough from the edges, and crimp or flute (see Vents, Appliqués, Crimps, Flutes, Lattice, pages 51–56).

6. Lightly brush some of the egg white wash over the entire pie, including the edges.

7. Bake for 20 minutes at 425°F (220°C). Reduce the heat to 350°F (175°C) and bake for 35 to 40 minutes more. When there are about 10 minutes of bake time left, open the oven, pull the pie out, and quickly and evenly sprinkle the top of the pie with sugar. Look for bubbling juice coming through the vents or latticework, and get your ear close to the top of the pie to hear the sizzle-whump (see Kate's Very Short Glossary of Pie-Making Terms on page 333).

8. Remove the pie from the oven and cool completely before serving so the filling can set up.

Apricot Pie

Ripe apricots signal the beginning of the summer stone fruit season. Two of my favorite varieties are Apache and Robada, which I mail order from Frog Hollow Farm. Both have a deep pink blush over their orange skins that make them look like a watercolor painting. Really sweet ones don't need much more than a squeeze of lemon and a grating of fresh nutmeg to highlight their flavor. Apricots should be juicy and sweet, not mealy and dry.

MAKES ONE 9-INCH DEEP-DISH PIE

INGREDIENTS
· · · · ·

6 cups (680–900 grams), about 1½–2 pounds, sweet, ripe apricots, pitted and quartered

½ cup (100 grams) sugar

A small grating of freshly ground nutmeg

⅓ teaspoon (2 grams) salt

1 teaspoon (5 grams) freshly squeezed lemon juice

⅓ cup (48 grams) flour

1–2 teaspoons (4–8 grams) quick-cooking tapioca

1 recipe double-crust pie dough

½ tablespoon (7 grams) butter

2 teaspoons (8 grams) sugar, for sprinkling on top of the pie

EGG WASH

1 egg white plus 1 tablespoon (15 grams) water, fork beaten

PROCEDURE

. . . . .

1. Preheat the oven to 425°F (220°C).

2. Put cut apricots, sugar, nutmeg, salt, lemon juice, flour, and tapioca in a big bowl and mix lightly.

3. Roll out the bottom dough and place it in your pie pan. Add the fruit filling and dot the top with little pieces of butter, if you remember.

4. Roll out the remaining dough, lay it over the fruit, and cut 5 to 6 vents on top, or cut strips and make a lattice top. Trim excess dough from the edges and crimp (see Vents, Appliqués, Crimps, Flutes, Lattice, pages 51–56).

5. Lightly brush some of the egg white wash over the entire pie, including the edges.

6. Bake for 15 minutes at 425°F (220°C). Reduce the heat to 375°F (190°C) and bake for 35 minutes. Ten to 15 minutes before end of the bake time, open the oven, pull the pie out, and quickly and evenly sprinkle the top of the pie with sugar. Close the oven and continue baking for another 10 to 15 minutes, until the top is golden brown and there is some steady bubbling and steaming coming through the vents.

7. Let cool before serving so the filling can set up.

Apricot Raspberry Pie

Apricots and raspberries mixed together make one of the prettiest fillings I have ever seen. I look forward to this one all year long and make a few to give away to very appreciative friends and neighbors.

MAKES ONE 9-INCH DEEP-DISH PIE

INGREDIENTS
. . . . .

4 cups (624 grams), about 1⅓ pounds, sweet, ripe apricots, pitted and quartered

2 cups (250 grams), about ½ pound, fresh or unthawed frozen raspberries

½ cup (100 grams) sugar, adjust for sweetness of fruit and to your taste

A small grating of freshly ground nutmeg

⅓ teaspoon (2 grams) salt

1 teaspoon (5 grams) freshly squeezed lemon juice

1–2 tablespoons (15–30 grams) Cointreau or other liqueur (optional)

⅓ cup (48 grams) flour

1–2 teaspoon (4–8 grams) quick-cooking tapioca

1 recipe double-crust pie dough

½ tablespoon (7 grams) butter

1–2 teaspoons (4–8 grams) sugar, for sprinkling on top of the pie

EGG WASH

1 egg white plus 1 tablespoon (15 grams) water, fork beaten

PROCEDURE

· · · · ·

1. Preheat the oven to 425 (220°C).

2. Put cut apricots, raspberries, sugar, nutmeg, salt, lemon juice, optional Cointreau, flour, and tapioca in a big bowl and mix lightly.

3. Roll out the bottom dough and place in your pie pan. Add fruit filling and dot the top with little pieces of butter. It's okay, if you forget. I do about 80 percent of the time.

4. Roll out remaining dough, lay over the fruit, and cut 5 to 6 vents on top, or cut strips and make a lattice top. Trim excess dough from the edges and crimp (see Vents, Appliqués, Crimps, Flutes, Lattice, pages 51–56).

5. Lightly brush some of the egg white wash over the entire pie, including the edges.

6. Bake for 15 minutes at 425°F (220°C). Reduce the heat to 375°F (190°C) and after about 45 minutes total time open the oven and quickly sprinkle the top of the pie with sugar. Close the oven and continue baking for another 10 to 15 minutes, or until you see steady bubbling in the filling coming through the vents or lattice. If the top of the pie looks like it is browning too quickly, cover the top of the pie with a piece of foil, turned shiny side down, with a vent torn in the middle.

7. Remove the pie from oven and cool completely so that the filling has a chance to set up.

Plum Pie

When Little Jack Horner stuck his thumb into the pie, it wasn't a tasty Santa Rosa plum that he pulled out. In early eighteenth-century England, important documents were sometimes hidden inside of baked pies so they could be safely transported to their final destination. One particular pie is believed to have held the deeds to a dozen English properties, one of which was a lead mine. When that pie arrived, rumor has it the deed to the lead mine was missing. Since plumbum is the Latin word for lead, perhaps Jack may have pulled out a rather special "plum" for himself.

MAKES ONE 9-INCH SHALLOW PIE

INGREDIENTS
· · · · ·

6 cups (680–900 grams), about 1½–2 pounds, Santa Rosa plums, pitted and quartered

¾ cup (150 grams) sugar

A small grating of freshly ground nutmeg

⅓ teaspoon (2 grams) salt

1–2 tablespoons (15–30 grams) Cointreau or other orange liqueur (optional)

⅓ cup (48 grams) flour

1 tablespoon (12 grams) quick-cooking tapioca

1 recipe double-crust pie dough

1 knob butter, about ½ tablespoon (7 grams)

1–2 teaspoons (4–8 grams) sugar, for sprinkling on top of the pie

EGG WASH

1 egg white plus 1 tablespoon (15 grams) water, fork beaten

CONTINUED

PROCEDURE

· · · · ·

1. Preheat the oven to 425°F (220°C).

2. In a medium bowl, place the plums, sugar, nutmeg, salt, Cointreau, flour, and tapioca, and mix until the fruit is well coated.

3. Pour the filling into an unbaked pie shell and dot with a small knob of butter cut into little pieces. It's okay to tear off pieces with your fingers, too.

4. Roll out the remaining dough, lay it over the fruit, and cut 5 to 6 vents on top, or cut strips and make a lattice top. Trim excess dough from the edges and crimp (see Vents, Appliqués, Crimps, Flutes, Lattice, pages 51–56).

5. Lightly brush some of the egg white wash over the entire pie, including the edges.

6. Bake for 20 minutes at 425°F (220°C). Reduce the heat to 350°F (175°C) and bake for 30 to 35 minutes more. When there are about 10 minutes of bake time left, open the oven, pull the pie out, and quickly and evenly sprinkle the top of the pie with sugar. If the filling is not making steady bubbles, turn the heat back up to 450°F (230°C) for 5 minutes to help it along. If needed, cover the pie loosely with a vented piece of aluminum foil, shiny side down, before you turn the heat up.

7. Remove the pie from oven and cool as long as you can before serving, so the filling can set up.

How to Organize a Homemade Pie Potluck

Three Weeks Ahead
· · · ·

Send out an invitation to friends who love to make, share, and eat pie, to join you for a Pie Potluck. In the RSVP, ask your guests to let you know what savory or sweet creation they will be bringing. For those who don't bake, suggest bringing ice cream, lemonade, a sparkling wine, or a salad to add to the table. Now sit back and wait for the replies to arrive in your Inbox.

One Week Out
· · · ·

Send out an email reminder for last-minute RSVPs. If you need an extra table, make arrangements, or use two sawhorses with an old door on top. Decide what pie(s) you will be making.

Two Days To Go
· · · ·

Make sure you have enough pie servers, plates, napkins, forks, glasses, and pitchers for lemonade and ice water. Check the weather report. Will this party be inside or out? Make your own dough ahead of time so it will be ready to roll.

The Day Before
· · · ·

Make and bake your pies so they are ready for the party. Make sure you have extra room in the freezer for ice cream, or in an ice chest with a bag of ice to keep things cool.

It's Pie Day
· · · ·

Cover your table with a pretty vintage cloth and add some seasonal flowers. Set out plates, forks, napkins, glasses, and pie servers. Have some paper and pens available on which your guests can write the name of the pie they have brought, ingredients for those with allergies, and who made it. Place your pies on the table. Turn on some music, take off your apron, and wait for the first arrival. Give out blue ribbons to each pie maker for bringing a pie.

Nectarine Pie

When you find fresh nectarines with pie-worthy flavor, make this pie. If you have a nectarine tree in your backyard, make a few more and give them away. Nectarines can be even sweeter than peaches.

MAKES ONE 9-INCH DEEP-DISH PIE

INGREDIENTS

· · · · ·

6 cups (680–900 grams), about 1½–2 pounds, ripe nectarines, halved, pitted, sliced, and chopped

¼–½ cup (50–100 grams) sugar—adjust for the sweetness of the fruit

A small pinch of fresh ground nutmeg, enough that you can smell it when you lean down to the bowl

1 teaspoon (5 grams) freshly squeezed lemon juice

⅓ teaspoon (2 grams) salt

⅓ cup (48 grams) flour

1 tablespoon (12 grams) quick-cooking tapioca

1 recipe double-crust pie dough

½ tablespoon (7 grams) butter

1–2 teaspoons (4–8 grams) sugar, for sprinkling on top of the pie

EGG WASH

1 egg white plus 1 tablespoon (15 grams) water, fork beaten

1. Preheat the oven to 425°F (220°C).
2. Place the nectarines, sugar, nutmeg, lemon juice, salt, flour, and quick-cooking tapioca in a big bowl. Mix lightly until the fruit is coated.
3. Roll out the bottom dough and place it in a pie pan.
4. Spoon in the fruit filling and dot with butter cut into little pieces with your fingers.
5. Roll out the remaining dough, lay it over the fruit, and cut 5 to 6 vents on top, or cut strips and make a lattice top. Trim excess dough from the edges and crimp (see Vents, Appliqués, Crimps, Flutes, Lattice, pages 51–56).
6. Lightly brush some of the egg white wash over the entire pie, including the edges.
7. Bake for 20 minutes at 425°F (220°C). Reduce the heat to 375°F (190°C) and after about 45 minutes total time, open the oven and quickly sprinkle the top of the pie with sugar. Close the oven and continue baking for another 10 to 15 minutes, or until you see steady bubbling in the filling coming through the vents or lattice.
8. Remove the pie from oven and cool as long as you can before serving, so the filling can set up.

· · · PIE-BYS, A PRACTICE OF GENEROSITY IN 3 EASY STEPS · · ·

1. Bake a pie.
2. Take still-warm pie to an unsuspecting friend's house.
3. Quietly leave pie where it will be found.

· ·

After dinner one evening, I decided that I would

muster up my courage and make a few pies for the county fair. By the time three pies—a blackberry, a peach, and a rhubarb—were out of the oven, it was well after midnight, and I was looking forward to getting some sleep. Just as I was turning off the kitchen light, I heard a little voice in my head say, "Make one more." It had to be kidding. There was no way I was going to make another. Sleep was calling and I was ready to lay my head on my pillow. "Make one more," the voice said again, stronger this time. "No, really . . . I'm tired," I thought back at it. "I need to sleep." But, when I heard "Kate! Make–One–More!" I resignedly turned the kitchen light back on, cranked up the oven, and, facing the baking counter, wondered what the heck I would make for this last pie that some as-yet-unnamed pie sprite commanded me to create. I don't often hear voices . . . really.

Up in my baking cupboard, there was a jar of home-canned Morello cherries that I had been given earlier in the summer. Hearing no objection from the pie sprite, I pulled them down from the shelf. I quickly put together a filling, rolled out another dough, placed it in the pan, and turned the red fruit mixture into it. Even though I was nearly asleep on my feet now, somehow I managed to make a pretty lattice top, too. I placed the pie in the oven, and then curled up on the couch figuring that my timer would alert me when it was time to check on it. But, in my somnambulistic state, I had forgotten to set the timer, and woke up to the unmistakable smell of the dreaded sugar burn. Oh no! My pie! Jumping up from the couch, I hurried to the oven, opened it, and was devastated to see that the tallest parts and edges of my pie had burned. At three o'clock in the morning, this was not a happy pie-making moment. I muttered a few choice words under my breath, but the pie sprite was not giving me any suggestions as to how I might save this

one. What to do? There on my counter lay a paring knife, and I wondered if I might just scrape off the dark patches with it, much like one would do with burnt toast. I didn't have much to lose, so I scraped gingerly and off came the sugar burn. Hallelujah. I brushed away the crumbs from the top of the pie with a pastry brush, checked that the oven was off, and gratefully collapsed on my bed. Anything else could wait until the morning, when things always seem to look better anyway.

When daylight came, I thought all four pies looked pretty darn good. I loaded each into a pie basket, carefully tucked them into the back of my car, and drove to the fairgrounds. I must have been quite a sight, walking in with baskets placed over each arm and in each hand. I filled out the entry forms, handed them over to the nice fair official who was in charge of the baking entries, and headed home. It would be a two-day wait before the results were announced, and I sincerely hoped the judges wouldn't be able to tell just how close to a complete disaster pie number four had come.

On fair day, I hurried straight to the home arts building. My blackberry, peach, and rhubarb pies each had blue ribbons but my cherry pie was nowhere to be seen. I had a sinking feeling that it may have been so bad that the judges simply tossed it out. The fair official who had registered my pies saw me repeatedly cruising the pie cases, bending down and looking, and looking some more. She asked if I needed some help. I told her I was looking for my cherry pie. "You might take a look on the other side of the case." I did. There it was. My cherry pie—with two ribbons: a first-prize blue, and the coveted green-and-white Best of Show! The pie sprite was right—that fourth pie was the perfect one to make. But maybe what it was really trying to show me in that late-night session was this: What happens between you and your pie stays between you and your pie.

PIE CONTESTS

It takes a lot of courage to put the labor of your heart and hands out on a table where it is picked apart and critiqued. I believe every homemade pie is a winner, so I would like to have pie contests where everyone is awarded a blue ribbon just for entering. Then let's create lots of categories: best crimping, best color, best lattice, best vents, best meringue topping, most beautiful pie pan, oldest pie pan, youngest baker, oldest baker, most creatively named pie . . . the list can go on and on.

In 2010, Gina Hyam interviewed me for her book *Pie Contest in a Box*. I told her that I dedicate each pie to a friend in need when I bake. This inspired her to come up with the idea of a pie contest "where everybody bakes their pie in honor of someone in your community who is struggling—whether they are facing cancer or unemployment or going through a difficult divorce—and invite that person to be the guest of honor at your party. If they are dealing with financial challenges, charge an entry fee and give the honoree the proceeds." She calls it "Pie Contest as Healing Force." Everybody wins with this one.

Sour Cherry Pie

When cherry season is full-on in July, I head to my favorite neighborhood sour pie cherry tree and pick flat after flat of shiny red sour cherries. I pit and freeze them in a single layer on sheet pans the same day, then transfer them to freezer bags so I can make sour cherry pies all year long, or at least until they run out. If you use frozen cherries, you won't need to defrost them when you make the filling or bake the pie. This recipe won me my first Best of Show ribbon.

A note on cherries: There is a difference between sweet cherries, like Bings and Rainiers, which are great for eating out of hand, and tart Montmorency and Morello cherries, which are known to make exceptional sour cherry pies. Sour cherries are slightly smaller and rounder than sweet cherries, ranging in color from the bright red Montmorency to the darker Morello. Generally you will find sour pie cherries in season at your farmers' market, and they are also used for commercial canned pie filling. You can make a pie with sweet cherries, but you will want to reduce the sugar to about ⅝ cup (125 grams) and add 2 teaspoons (10 grams) of lemon juice to give it a bright flavor. Cherries are extremely juicy, so don't skimp on the thickener. I use quick-cooking tapioca in this pie, which also helps keep the filling looking clear and shiny.

MAKES ONE 9-INCH DEEP-DISH PIE

· · · · · · · · · · · · · · · · **NOTE** · · · · · · · · · · · · · · ·

Trader Joe's carries jars of Morello sour cherries. Be sure to drain them well before using. Costco carries bags of tart cherries in the freezer section.

· ·

CONTINUED

INGREDIENTS

· · · · ·

6 cups (680–900 grams), about 1½–2 pounds, pitted sour pie cherries, drained, fresh or unthawed frozen

1 cup (200 grams) sugar

1 teaspoon (5 grams) freshly squeezed lemon juice

A very small grating of nutmeg

⅓ teaspoon (2 grams) salt

1 tablespoon (15 grams) Cointreau or other orange liqueur

3 tablespoons (36 grams) quick-cooking tapioca

1 recipe double-crust pie dough

½ tablespoon (7 grams) butter

1–2 teaspoons (4–8 grams) sugar, for sprinkling on top of the pie

EGG WASH

1 egg white plus 1 tablespoon (15 grams) water, fork beaten

PROCEDURE

· · · · ·

1. Preheat the oven to 425°F (220°C).

2. Place the sour pie cherries, sugar, lemon juice, nutmeg, salt, Cointreau, and quick-cooking tapioca into a big bowl, and mix until the fruit looks like it is coated with coarse wet sand.

3. Pour the filling into a chilled crust and dot the top with the remaining butter. Place the pie in the fridge.

4. Roll out the remaining dough, lay it over the fruit, and cut 5 to 6 vents on top, or cut strips and make a lattice top. Trim excess dough from the edges and crimp (see Vents, Appliqués, Crimps, Flutes, Lattice, pages 51–56).

5. Lightly brush some of the egg white wash over the entire pie, including the edges.

6. Bake for 20 minutes at 425°F (220°C). Reduce the heat to 375°F (190°C) and after about 45 minutes total time, open the oven and quickly sprinkle the top of the pie with sugar. Close the oven and continue baking for another 10 to 15 minutes, or until you see steady bubbling in the filling coming through the vents or lattice. If you don't see the steady bubbling, cover the pie loosely with foil, turn up the oven the 445°F (230°C), and bake for an additional 5 to 6 minutes. You are letting your pie know it is time to finish up, NOW!

7. Remove the pie from the oven and cool completely so that the filling has a chance to set up.

Cranberry Pie

Try this cranberry pie in the fall or winter when you are craving the bright taste of a sour cherry pie. Add pecans to this filling if you'd like, as well as some orange zest or liqueur, and serve it with champagne. There is a lot of naturally occurring pectin in cranberries, so not much thickener is needed.

MAKES ONE 9-INCH SHALLOW PIE

INGREDIENTS
· · · · ·

1 quart, about 4 cups (396 grams), whole cranberries, fresh or unthawed frozen, divided

1¼ cups (250 grams) sugar

2½ teaspoons (6 grams) cornstarch

A pinch or small grating of freshly ground nutmeg

¼ teaspoon (a pinch) salt

½ teaspoon fresh orange zest or 1 tablespoon (15 grams) orange liqueur

½ cup (60 grams) chopped walnuts (optional)

1 recipe double-crust pie dough

1 knob butter, the size of a small walnut, cut into small pieces for dotting the top of the filling

1–2 teaspoons (4–8 grams) sugar, for sprinkling on top of the pie

EGG WASH

1 egg white plus 1 tablespoon (15 grams) water, fork beaten

CONTINUED

PROCEDURE

· · · · ·

1. Place 3 cups of the cranberries in a food processor and pulse until they are slightly chopped. In a medium bowl, place the chopped and remaining whole cranberries, sugar, cornstarch, nutmeg, salt, zest or liqueur, and optional walnuts, and mix well.

2. In a pie plate lined with an unbaked pie dough, pour in the cranberry filling and dot with butter.

3. Roll out the remaining dough, lay it over the fruit, and cut 5 to 6 vents on top, or cut strips and make a lattice top. Trim excess dough from the edges and crimp (see Vents, Appliqués, Crimps, Flutes, Lattice, pages 51–56).

4. Chill the pie for a minimum of 1 hour before baking.

5. Lightly brush some of the egg white wash over the entire pie, including the edges.

6. In an oven preheated to 375°F (190°C), bake on the middle rack for about 40 minutes. When there are about 10 minutes of bake time left, open the oven, pull the pie out, and quickly and evenly sprinkle the top of the pie with sugar. Close the oven and bake until the crust is just golden, or until you see steady bubbling coming out between the vents.

7. Remove the pie from the oven and cool completely before serving.

· · · · · · · · · · · PIE DAYS TO CELEBRATE · · · · · · · · · · ·

I didn't pick these dates and you can pick any day to be a special pie day.

JAN 23 National Pie Day and Rhubarb Pie Day

FEBRUARY Great American Pie Month

FEB 20 Cherry Pie Day

FIRST FULL WEEK OF MARCH British Pie Week

MAR 2 Banana Cream Pie Day

MAR 14 Pi Day

APR 28 Blueberry Pie Day

MAY 8 Coconut Cream Pie Day

MAY 13 Apple Pie Day

JUN 9 Strawberry-Rhubarb Pie Day

JUL 12 Pecan Pie Day

AUG 1 Raspberry Cream Pie Day

AUG 15 Lemon Meringue Pie Day

AUG 18 Ice Cream Pie Day

AUG 20 Chocolate Pecan Pie Day

AUG 24 Peach Pie Day

SEPT 28 Strawberry Cream Pie Day

OCT 12 Pumpkin Pie Day

OCT 23 Boston Cream Pie Day

OCT 26 National Mincemeat Pie Day

NOV 27 Bavarian Cream Pie Day

DEC 1 National Pie Day

DEC 1 National Fried Pie Day

DEC 25 Pumpkin Pie Day

· ·

CHAPTER SIX

Old-Fashioned Rhubarb and Citrus Pies

In 2009 I was filmed making pie with *Gourmet*

magazine's last editor-in-chief, Ruth Reichl. Ruth has been making pies all her life, and I hoped that my own dough would be up to her very high standards, as she is one of my all-time food heroes. I never thought that finding the right kitchen for the shoot would turn out to be more stressful than actually making the pies. I would have loved to film in the funky old Seattle house where I was living, but the kitchen layout wasn't quite right. My next try, the sleek and modern-ish kitchen of friends, was also a no-go after I could not get their oven to cooperate over two full days of test baking. I wish I had known that this challenge could easily have been solved by simply pre-baking a few pies at home, and pulling them out of the oven with a flourish when it was time for the big finish. But not knowing this and with less than twenty-four hours to go, I was racking my brain for another spot. Dear friends of mine, Jeanette and Andrew, had a charming vintage kitchen, so with fingers and lattice strips crossed, I called to ask if it would be possible for me to completely take over their house the following afternoon for this once-in-a-lifetime project. Their answer: "Absolutely, we would love to do that!" I piled my traveling pie kit back into my car and drove right over to make two more test pies. When I arrived, Andrew helped carry my gear inside, gave me the lay of the land, and left me to my work.

Jeanette and Andrew's kitchen epitomizes an old-fashioned scene straight out of *Our Town*. The two sash windows over the farmhouse sink that look out to their lush garden give it a light and airy feel, plus their reconditioned 1943 double-oven range, on which everything still works (including the timer bell), is the kind I dream of owning someday. I had already made a dozen test pies, so the two I made in their kitchen would bring the number up to fourteen. They went together easily and I set them in the ovens for the bake. As if on cue, the production team walked into the kitchen, now heavily scented by freshly baking apple pies, and watched as I pulled out two golden-domed beauties. The crew agreed that the set was "perfectly charming," and I let out a big sigh of relief while dishing up slices for them to

try. After second helpings, they asked if I might be able to bring some colorful items of my own to personalize the space a bit more, so the next morning I collected a few wooden spoons, crockery bowls, dented metal measuring cups, and even the lace curtains from my kitchen. There was one last thing I knew I needed for luck. Over the baking counter in my Pie Cottage kitchen I have a framed fruit crate label of a shamrock, and Merrilyn, my next-door neighbor in Seattle, has the very same one. Just before leaving for filming, I ran up the walk and knocked on her door, hoping to borrow it. Without a blink of the eye, she turned to fetch it, and handed it to me to take along with a hug. Now I was ready to go.

Ruth was already there when I arrived, looking calm like the consummate professional she is. I brought my baskets and boxes into the mudroom—now the staging area—and quickly found places on "the set" for Merrilyn's shamrock and my other "props." I put on a new apron I had made, was wired for sound, shared a smile and hug with Ruth, and we started in on our pies: an apple and a rhubarb—numbers fifteen and sixteen. Side by side, we made dough and chatted about ingredients and technique. We agreed on many things. For example, we both make our dough a bit on the moist side so it will hold together and roll out more easily, and in a double-crust pie, we each make one disc of dough larger, but while Ruth uses her larger dough for the bottom crust, I use mine for the top, so that there will be extra in case any patching is needed.

I had brought beautiful crimson stalks of rhubarb that were almost two inches wide. I wish I had said something a bit more stellar than, "Yeah, we grow some pretty big rhubarb up here in the Northwest" when Ruth marveled at their size. Along with supplying the largest percentage of the nation's rhubarb crop, Washington State rhubarb farmers grow big stalks. We used two of my favorite apple varieties—Newtown Pippin and Golden Russet—for a combination I knew would make a pie filling both sweet and tart. When I pulled out my vintage 1963 Veg-O-Matic for slicing them, a really big grin spread over Ruth's face and she said, "You're kidding!" Ruth was totally game to try this old tool

and quickly saw how it makes just the right sized slices for an apple pie in no time at all. We seasoned and assembled our pies, dotted them with butter, placed the dough on top, and shared our favorite ways to finish the edges: Ruth's were finger-fluted, and mine were crimped with a fork like Geeg had taught me. After a quick egg white wash and a sprinkling of sugar, we set them to bake in the oven. Success. I had baked another two pies at home that morning just in case something went wrong, so instead of waiting for ours to finish baking, the crew had us swap them out with my pre-baked ones. The camera zoomed in on our oven mitted-hands pulling two pies from the oven, and that concluded the day's filming. The producers were happy. Ruth was happy. Andrew and Jeanette were happy. And I was very happy, and greatly relieved that everything had gone off without a hitch.

Before she left the house, Ruth pulled me aside and said, "Kate, your approach to baking has been so liberating for me. You break all the rules and it comes out great every time." The footage of our baking session ended up not being used, but that is a small matter because I've got a feature-length film of a very special day that I can call up at any time from my memory bank. For me, making pie with Ruth Reichl will always be a treasured experience. And those lace curtains? I left them with Jeanette and Andrew. They were perfect over the windows.

Old-Fashioned Rhubarb Pie

This is the pie your grandmother made with rhubarb she picked from her garden, and boy is it good. I watch in the early spring for the first signs of leaves unfurling on the rhubarb plants in my garden, and when the stalks are big and red a few weeks later, I pull the first rhubarb pie of the season out of the oven. Rhubarb is also known as pie plant.

MAKES ONE 9-INCH DEEP-DISH PIE

INGREDIENTS
· · · · ·

7–8 cups (875–1000 grams), 1¾–2 pounds, fresh or unthawed frozen rhubarb, cut into ½–1-inch (1.5–3 centimeters) pieces

1⅓ cups (167 grams) granulated sugar

A small pinch of ground nutmeg

½ teaspoon (3 grams) freshly squeezed lemon juice

⅓ teaspoon (2 grams) salt

½ cup (73 grams) flour

2 teaspoons (8 grams) quick-cooking tapioca

1 recipe double-crust pie dough

½ tablespoon (7 grams) butter

1 tablespoon (12 grams) sugar for sprinkling on top

EGG WASH

1 egg white plus 1 tablespoon (15 grams) water, fork beaten

CONTINUED

HOW TO HARVEST RHUBARB

Sumner, Washington is the Rhubarb Pie Capital of the World—well, the self-proclaimed capital—and farmer Ron Leslie's family has been growing it there for three generations. The farms in this area grow the majority of rhubarb for the entire United States. I didn't know this until I was invited to visit to the farm.

As soon as I arrived, Farmer Ron walked me out into rows and rows of the lush green leaves of his rhubarb fields that went all the way to the hills in the distance. He stopped to pull back some of the colossal leaves so I could see thick bright red stalks, fourteen inches tall and more, attached to the crown of the plants. Then he bent over to reach way down inside the plant to the crown, grabbed hold of an individual stalk, and tugged straight up, cleanly separating the stalk from the plant. Farmer Ron said that if you don't pull straight up, chances are you'll break the stalk. Under his tutelage, I gave it a try and pulled up a big red stalk of my own completely intact. He took it from my hand, held it parallel to the ground, and taking a knife from his pocket, neatly trimmed off most all of the leafy end, as well as the crown end that moments before had been attached to the plant. That's how the stalks are cut and packed for shipping. He presented me with another big red stalk with fanned leaf on top and I felt like pie royalty as I carried it around like a scepter.

PROCEDURE

· · · · ·

1. Preheat the oven to 450°F (230°C).

2. Place the rhubarb, sugar, nutmeg, lemon juice, salt, flour, and tapioca in a big bowl, and mix until the rhubarb looks like it is coated with coarse wet sand.

3. Roll out the bottom dough and place in pie pan.

4. Heap the filling over the dough in a pie plate and dot with butter broken into little pieces with your fingers.

5. Roll out the remaining dough, lay it over the fruit, and cut 5 to 6 vents on top, or cut strips and make a lattice top. Trim excess dough from the edges and crimp (see Vents, Appliqués, Crimps, Flutes, Lattice, pages 51–56).

6. Lightly brush some of the egg white wash over the entire pie, including the edges.

7. Bake for 15 minutes at 450°F (230°C). Reduce the heat to 350°F (175°C) and after about 45 minutes total time, open the oven and quickly sprinkle the top of the pie with sugar. Close the oven and continue baking for another 10 to 15 minutes, or until you see steady bubbling in the filling coming through the vents or lattice.

8. Remove the pie from the oven and cool completely before serving. The longer it cools, the better it sets up, and the less runny it will be.

· **NOTE** · · · · · · · · · · · · · · · · ·

Don't worry if you forget to sprinkle on the sugar during the last part of the bake. Sprinkle it on as soon as it comes out of the oven.

· ·

Strawberry Rhubarb Pie

This classic pie uses one part strawberry to two parts rhubarb. You don't have to be too exact in the proportions. Try "measuring" fresh or unthawed frozen fruit directly into the pie pan to the height of one half inch below the rim. If you mound it up more, it will boil over during the bake.

MAKES ONE 9-INCH DEEP-DISH PIE

INGREDIENTS

· · · · ·

1–2 cups (113–227 grams), ¼–½ pound, fresh or unthawed frozen strawberries, sliced if large

5 cups (625 grams), about 1¼ pounds, fresh or unthawed frozen rhubarb cut into ½–1-inch (1.5–3 centimeters) size pieces

1 cup (200 grams) sugar

½ teaspoon freshly squeezed lemon juice

Tiny pinch or grating of fresh nutmeg

⅓ teaspoon (2 grams) salt

2 tablespoons (24 grams) quick-cooking tapioca

¼ cup (36 grams) flour

1 recipe double-crust pie dough

½ tablespoon (7 grams) butter, more if you like

1 tablespoon (12 grams) sugar for sprinkling on top

EGG WASH

1 egg white plus 1 tablespoon (15 grams) water, fork beaten

PROCEDURE

· · · · ·

1. Preheat the oven to 425°F (220°C).

2. Fill a 9-inch deep-dish pie pan with 1 part strawberries and 2 parts rhubarb so that it comes to about ½ inch below the top of the pie pan.

3. Pour the fruit into a medium bowl. Rinse and wipe dry the pie pan you used to measure the fruit, and set in the fridge to chill.

4. Add the sugar, lemon juice, nutmeg, salt, tapioca, and flour to the bowl of fruit, and mix with a spoon until the fruit is coated well.

5. Roll out the bottom dough and place in the pie pan.

6. Spoon in the fruit filling, and dot with butter broken into little pieces with your fingers.

7. Roll out remaining dough, lay over the fruit, and cut 5 to 6 vents on top, or cut strips and make a lattice top. Trim excess dough from the edges and crimp (see Vents, Appliqués, Crimps, Flutes, Lattice, pages 51–56).

8. Lightly brush some of the egg white wash over the entire pie, including the edges.

9. Bake for 20 minutes. Reduce the heat to 375°F (190°C) and after about 45 minutes total time, open the oven and quickly sprinkle the top of the pie with sugar. Close the oven and continue baking for another 10 to 15 minutes, or until you see steady bubbling in the filling coming through the vents or lattice.

10. Remove the pie from the oven and cool completely before serving. The longer the pie cools, the better it will set up, and the less runny it will be.

Raspberry Rhubarb Pie

Here's a delicious spin on the strawberry rhubarb pie it is modeled after. I use two parts rhubarb and one part raspberry. Add a favorite liqueur and the flavor really pops.

MAKES ONE 9-INCH SHALLOW PIE

INGREDIENTS

· · · · ·

2½ cups (312 grams) rhubarb, about ¾ pound, cut into ½–1-inch (1.5–3 centimeters) pieces, fresh or unthawed frozen

1½ cups (187 grams), about 6–7 ounces, raspberries, fresh or unthawed frozen

¾ cup (150 grams) sugar

A grating or two of fresh nutmeg

½ teaspoon freshly squeezed lemon juice

⅓ teaspoon (2 grams) salt

1 tablespoon (15 grams) liqueur of your choice—orange, raspberry, or lemon work well

1½ tablespoons (18 grams) quick-cooking tapioca

2 tablespoons (16 grams) all-purpose flour

1 recipe double-crust pie dough

½ tablespoon (7 grams) butter, more if you like

1 tablespoon (12 grams) sugar, for sprinkling on top of the pie

EGG WASH

1 egg white plus 1 tablespoon (15 grams) water, fork beaten

CONTINUED

PROCEDURE

· · · · ·

1. Preheat the oven to 425°F (220°C).
2. In medium bowl, combine the rhubarb, raspberries, sugar, nutmeg, lemon juice, salt, optional liqueur, quick-cooking tapioca, and flour. Toss to coat the fruit.
3. Roll out bottom pie dough and place in pan.
4. Pour the filling into the piecrust. Top with butter broken into small pieces with your fingers.
5. Roll out the remaining dough, lay it over the fruit, and cut 5 to 6 vents on top, or cut strips and make a lattice top. Trim excess dough from the edges and crimp (see Vents, Appliqués, Crimps, Flutes, Lattice, pages 51–56).
6. Lightly brush some of the egg white wash over the entire pie, including the edges.
7. Bake for 20 minutes at 425°F (220°C). Reduce the heat to 375°F (190°C) and after about 45 minutes total time, open the oven and quickly sprinkle the top of the pie with sugar. Close the oven and continue baking for another 10 to 15 minutes, or until you see steady bubbling in the filling coming through the vents or lattice.
8. Remove the pie from the oven and let it cool completely, or as long as you can, before serving. The longer it cools, the better it sets up, and the less runny it will be.

· · · · · · · · · · · · · · · · · · **NOTE** · · · · · · · · · · · · · · · · · ·

If using a larger pie pan, increase the amounts of all ingredients proportionately, but stay about one-half inch below the rim so the filling will not boil over onto the floor of your oven.

· ·

Rhuberry Bluebarb Pie

I made a lot of these pies traveling down the West Coast one spring. Each town I visited had different berries available and I picked the sweetest to add to the rhubarb. It will take about 1¾ pounds (783 grams) fruit for this pie, but it's always nice to buy a little extra for tasting and "quality control."

MAKES ONE 9-INCH SHALLOW-DISH PIE

INGREDIENTS
· · · · ·

2½ cups (312 grams) rhubarb, about ¾ pound, cut into ½–1-inch (1.5–3 centimeters) pieces, fresh or unthawed frozen

1½ cups (226 grams), about ½ pound, blueberries or blackberries, fresh or unthawed frozen

A generous ¾ cup (150 grams) sugar, plus 1 tablespoon (12 grams) more for sprinkling on top of the pie

2 tablespoons (16 grams) all-purpose flour

A grating or two of nutmeg

1 teaspoon (6 grams) freshly squeezed lemon juice

⅓ teaspoon (2 grams) salt

2 tablespoons (24 grams) quick-cooking tapioca

1 recipe double-crust pie dough

½ tablespoon (7 grams) butter, more if you like

1 tablespoon (12 grams) sugar, for sprinkling on top of the pie

EGG WASH

1 egg white plus 1 tablespoon (15 grams) water, fork beaten

CONTINUED

PROCEDURE

·····

1. Preheat the oven to 425°F (220°C).
2. Roll out the pie dough and place it in a pie pan.
3. In a medium bowl, combine the rhubarb, blueberries or blackberries, sugar, flour, nutmeg, lemon juice, salt, and optional liqueur. Toss to coat the fruit and turn into waiting pie dough.
4. Roll out the remaining dough, lay it over the fruit, and cut 5 to 6 vents on top, or cut strips and make a lattice top. Trim excess dough from the edges and crimp (see Vents, Appliqués, Crimps, Flutes, Lattice, pages 51–56).
5. Lightly brush some of the egg white wash over the entire pie, including the edges.
6. Bake for 20 minutes. Reduce the heat to 375°F (190°C) and after about 45 minutes total time, open the oven and quickly sprinkle the top of the pie with sugar. Close the oven and continue baking for another 10 to 15 minutes, or until you see steady bubbling in the filling coming through the vents or lattice.
7. Remove the pie from the oven and let it cool completely before serving.

· · · · · · · · · · · · · · · · · · · NOTE · · · · · · · · · · · · · · · · · ·

Add 1 tablespoon (15 grams) liqueur of your choice—
orange, raspberry, or lemon work well.

· ·

Rhubarb Custard Pie

When the utility men in my little town knocked on my door to let me know that my water would be off while they replaced the meter, I let them know there would be freshly baked pie ready to share when they were done. Never ones to turn down that kind of offer, an hour later they knocked and sat down at my table while I dished up warm slices of Rhubarb Custard Pie. They must have liked it a lot because when they left, the pie plate was empty.

MAKES ONE 9-INCH SHALLOW DISH PIE PAN

INGREDIENTS
· · · · ·

1 recipe single-crust pie dough

2½ cups (312 grams) rhubarb, about ¾ pound, cut into ½–1-inch (1.5–3 centimeters) pieces, fresh or unthawed frozen

¾–1 cup (150–200 grams) granulated sugar, depending how sweet you like it

3 tablespoons (24 grams) flour, about 1 handful for me

1 teaspoon (5 grams) freshly squeezed lemon juice

⅛ teaspoon freshly ground nutmeg

¼ teaspoon (a pinch) salt

1 tablespoon (15 grams) orange liqueur (optional)

3 large eggs

1 cup (250 grams) whipping cream or half-and-half

2 tablespoons (30 grams) butter, melted

1–2 tablespoons (15–30 grams) sugar

¼ cup (30 grams) candied pecans (optional)

PROCEDURE

· · · · ·

1. Preheat oven to 400°F (205°C).
2. Roll out a pie dough and place it in a pie pan. Finish the edges with a flute or crimp. Cover the pan and place it in the fridge.
3. In a medium bowl, combine the rhubarb, sugar, flour, lemon juice, nutmeg, salt, and optional liqueur. Toss to coat the fruit and turn the filling into the piecrust.
4. Bake for 20 minutes.
5. Fork beat eggs in a small bowl, add whipping cream or half-and-half and melted butter, and stir to combine. Open the oven and carefully pour the mixture over the rhubarb baking in the pan.
6. Bake for 10 minutes more, or until the jiggle in the middle is about the size of a 50-cent piece (about 30 centimeters) and the custard is lightly browned on top.
7. Remove the pie from the oven. Sprinkle lightly with the remaining sugar and top with optional candied pecans.
8. Cool the pie before serving, although it is darn good served warm, too!

Lemon Meringue Pie

From the time I was little, I remember my grandmother's lemon meringue pie and how a slice of it could make you feel that everything was going to be all right when you were down. Geeg's pie was sweet without being too sweet, and tart without being too tart. She put on just enough meringue so that it wasn't top-heavy. Her pie was the star of the dessert table at all our family gatherings, and she was our Lemon Meringue Queen. Make the meringue immediately after the lemon filling goes into the pie pan and place it on top of a hot filling. This will help with weeping and shrinkage.

MAKES ONE 9-INCH SHALLOW PIE

INGREDIENTS
· · · · ·

3 egg yolks, fork beaten

1 cup (200 grams) sugar

⅓ cup (40 grams) cornstarch

A pinch of salt

1¼ cups (310 grams) warm water

1 tablespoon (14 grams) butter

½ cup (118 grams) freshly squeezed lemon juice

Zest of 1 large lemon

1 blind baked pie crust (see page 98)

1 recipe Meringue (recipe follows)

PROCEDURE

· · · · ·

1. In a small bowl, fork beat the egg yolks, and set them aside.

2. In a saucepan, combine the sugar, cornstarch and salt.

3. Add the water and, while constantly stirring with a whisk, bring the mixture to a boil. Reduce the heat and cook for 2 to 3 more minutes while continuing to whisk. Don't be afraid to whisk vigorously as it gets thicker.

4. Take ¼ cup of the hot mixture and stir it into the fork-beaten egg yolks. Return this to the saucepan and, while stirring, cook for 2 more minutes or until the mixture is thick.

5. Stir in the butter, lemon juice, and zest, and cook for another minute.

6. Immediately pour the mixture into the pre-baked piecrust and set aside.

7. Preheat the oven to 375°F (190°C) and make the meringue (recipe follows).

8. Put the meringue on the hot lemon filling starting at the edges first. Make sure the meringue reaches all the way to the edge of the crust so there are no gaps. Then add the rest of the meringue in the middle so that the filling is completely covered. Pull up some soft peaks with the handle of a spoon or the blade of a knife.

9. Place the pie in a preheated 375°F (190°C) oven for 6 minutes or until the peaks turn light brown.

10. Remove the pie from oven and let it cool completely before serving.

CONTINUED

Meringue

5 egg whites

A pinch of salt

⅓ cup (33 grams) sugar

⅛ teaspoon cream of tartar

MERINGUE PROCEDURE
· · · · ·

1. In a clean and cold bowl, beat the egg whites with an electric hand-held beater or a stand mixer.
2. Add the pinch of salt and the sugar while you mix. Add the cream of tartar and mix a bit more. Lift the beaters out when you can see soft peaks in thick foamy waves. That's when it's done.

· · · · · · · · · · · · · · · MAKING MERINGUE · · · · · · · · · · · · · ·

Geeg didn't have an electric hand mixer for a long time so
she whipped her egg whites with a hand-cranked beater.

· ·

Shaker Lemon Pie

If bright lemon marmalade makes your mouth sing, this pie is for you. There are only four ingredients in the filling, and the instructions are so easy that after making it once, you'll probably be able to make it again without needing to refer to the recipe. The whole lemon, rind and all, is sliced very finely and used. Some find the marmalade texture of the filling different from anything they've had before. If this is not your cup of tea, after thinly slicing the lemon, chop it finely with a knife before covering with sugar. I prefer to use Meyer lemons when in season, but any fresh thin-skinned lemon will do. I've made this pie open face and also with a full top. Bake time is the same for both. A scoop of vanilla ice cream or some homemade crème fraîche is very good with this pie.

MAKES ONE 9-INCH DEEP-DISH PIE OR FOUR 5-INCH MINI PIES

INGREDIENTS
· · · · ·

2 or 3 lemons

2 cups (400 grams) sugar

4 eggs, fork beaten well

Tiny pinch of salt

1 recipe single-crust pie dough

PROCEDURE

· · · · ·

1. Slice the lemons as thin as possible—the thinner the better. If you are comfortable using a mandolin, this is a good time to use it, but please watch your fingers!

2. Place the thin slices of lemon and their juices in a bowl with sugar. Mix with a spoon and let them sit overnight or at least 6 hours in the refrigerator.

3. When you are ready to make your pie, preheat the oven to 450°F (230°C).

4. Take the lemons and sugar out of the fridge and add the beaten eggs and the salt, and mix well.

5. Roll out the dough and place it in a pie pan, then pour in the filling.

6. Bake for 15 minutes and then reduce the heat to 375°F (190°C) for about 25 minutes more, but check it at 20 minutes. The pie is done when a knife inserted comes out clean.

Shaker Blood Orange Pie

Its better-known sister, Shaker Lemon, is like a glass of freshly made lemonade, but this version made with blood oranges is reminiscent of the smoother taste of orange sherbet. Adding one half lemon gives it just the right amount of zing. Slice the fruit with a sharp knife or mandolin, and chop finely before covering with sugar.

MAKES ONE 9-INCH DEEP-DISH PIE OR FOUR 5-INCH MINI PIES

INGREDIENTS
. . . . .

2 small blood oranges

½ lemon (thin skinned is best)

2 cups (400 grams) sugar

4 large eggs

A small pinch of salt

A tiny pinch of freshly ground nutmeg (optional)

1 recipe double-crust pie dough

EGG WASH

1 egg white plus 1 tablespoon (15 grams) water, fork beaten

1. Slice the oranges and lemon as thinly as possible. Place in a bowl with sugar. Mix with a spoon and let them sit overnight or at least 6 hours in the refrigerator.

2. When you are ready to make your pie, preheat the oven to 450°F (230°C).

3. Put the orange/lemon/sugar mixture in a fine-mesh sieve over a bowl and let the juice drip through.

4. Combine the juice, eggs, salt, and optional nutmeg and beat with a handheld mixer until light colored, about 3 minutes.

5. Add the chilled sugar/citrus mixture and stir until well combined, then set aside.

6. Roll out the bottom crust and place it in a pie pan, then pour in the filling.

7. Roll out the top crust, cover, seal, and crimp the edges.

8. Brush the pie lightly with egg white wash, and, just before you put it in the oven, cut a few vents. Don't worry if the filling comes through a bit.

9. Bake for 15 minutes and then reduce the heat to 375°F (190°C) for about 25 minutes more. When there are about 10 minutes of bake time left, open the oven, pull the pie out, and quickly and evenly sprinkle the top of the pie with sugar. Continue to bake for the remaining time and cool the pie completely before serving.

CHAPTER SEVEN

Creamy, Nutty, Cool, and Yummy

My mom was never known for her culinary prowess, and many, if not most, of our "homemade" meals had to be quick and easy for her to prepare because of her busy schedule as a music teacher. Our standard suppertime fare often consisted of variations of ground round, something green that was boiled to a mush, and instant rice or mashed potatoes from a box. The one cookbook she occasionally dipped into was her blue plaid-covered 1940s wartime edition of *The Joy of Cooking* that she had received as a bride. I recall her making three recipes from it: Red Devil's Food Cake with a 7-Minute White Icing, Chocolate Fudge that we took turns beating with a spoon in a metal bowl until our arms ached, and Plain Cake Doughnuts made only once. Out of the blue, she decided to make doughnuts one day, and I was overjoyed since we would be together in the kitchen, already my favorite place at age six.

The recipe in the cookbook called for optional cinnamon and nutmeg. Our cupboard had a box of cinnamon on the shelf reserved for my grandmother's pies. But nutmeg? That would need to be added to the grocery order Mom called in to our neighborhood market. We drove to pick it up a few hours later, and when we got home, Mom opened up the top of a small red cardboard box and I experienced my first scent of a spice that, for our household, was exotic. Into the batter it went. We used a doughnut hole cutter to make both rings and holes, and set all the shapes onto Melmac plates covered with wax paper. Then, one by one, Mom carefully slipped the doughnuts and holes into a big silver Revere Ware pot full of hot bubbling oil. I watched as their color turned from white to tan to brown. I still have the tongs in the shape of two hands that clap together—we called them "the happy hands." She used them to lift the hot doughnuts, dripping with fat, out of the pot and onto a newspaper-covered rack to drain and cool. We rolled and sprinkled them with sugar and, when they were cool enough to touch, shared them together. The kitchen was warm and fragrant like a bakery and I was happy with my mommy.

As I grew older, times like these were fewer. In 1963 we moved from the little white house next to Daddy's business to the house of my parents' dreams. When they signed the final papers, Daddy jokingly said that he would have to be carried out of it feet first. A few months later, on a sunny day in the fall, he had a bad fall and a blood clot travelled from his leg and lodged in his left lung. Hospitals. Doctors. Hushed voices. Overnight I felt the magic of my protected childhood wrenched away. A silence replaced the sunny disposition of my little girl years and the unspoken fear that his prophecy might come true was always there. Geeg swooped in to oversee the day-to-day goings-on in our house and make meals until things were on a more even keel. My dad never fully recovered and six years later, when I was sixteen, he passed away from a rare form of leukemia only ten days after my parents received the diagnosis. I pulled inward even more, and Mom, who had lost the love of her life, tried hard to keep some kind of open communication between us in whatever way she could during my sullen teenage silence.

I loved to walk, and she would ask to join me, knowing it was a way for us to spend time together without me having to say much. She would strap on her "flatties" and we would set off for a vigorous stretch of the leg. We climbed up and down the lower part of the Santa Barbara Riviera while she shared a few stories of her youth in an effort to encourage me to communicate. Like many teenage girls, I was the center and tragic heroine of my own personal drama. On one walk she pointed out six bungalows and cottages within just three blocks, all of which she had lived in as a little girl. It was news to me that my grandmother had moved her two young children every six months or so. As a single mom with an absentee husband, Geeg packed up her two babies in 1919 and singlehandedly navigated the one-lane road across the Colorado Rockies in an old Chevrolet to what she hoped would be a better future for all of them in California. I had no idea how much of a gypsy my grandmother had been until those walks. Along with Geeg's rolling pin, I may have picked up some of that same restlessness,

since I have also moved more times than I care to remember.

One year Mom was asked to provide two recipes for the special Fiesta edition of our local paper. She had no recipes of her own and knew full well that she wasn't a particularly good cook. She fretted and stewed over what contribution she could make that would not cause her or our family embarrassment. The calm and collected behavior befitting a lady that she modeled for me seemed to disappear with the stress of the approaching deadline. After consulting some of her music teacher colleagues—Lillian who did her hair every Friday, and Sadie right next door—she settled on one of the meals we ate on Friday nights: tuna-stuffed French rolls, and a tomato soup that my brother swears to this day she never actually made.

Mom did make a great grasshopper pie, though, that was very popular during the 1950s. It would have been a fine addition to the recipe column, but she may have decided against it since it contained two different liqueurs. Neither of my parents drank, which greatly pleased our teetotaling grandmother. Geeg adamantly believed that even one small sip of wine was the undeniable sign of a true and total alcoholic, and told us so on many occasions. But the nightly ration of crème de menthe that she poured for herself before bed? Well, that was purely for digestive purposes.

Grasshopper Pie

This very retro pie from the 1950s requires no rolling or baking. My mom made it for us on special occasions and I still love its mint green color and flavor. To garnish, save some chocolate cookie crumbs to sprinkle on top.

MAKES ONE 9-INCH SHALLOW PIE

INGREDIENTS
· · · · ·

24 regular marshmallows

⅔ cup (161 grams) half-and-half

2 tablespoons (30 grams) each, crème de cacao and crème de menthe

½ pint (232 grams) plus 4 tablespoons (60 grams) whipping cream, divided

1 recipe Chocolate Cookie Crumb Crust (page 94), chilled

1 teaspoon (3 grams) finely ground chocolate cookie crumbs

1–2 mint sprigs, for garnish

PROCEDURE
· · · · ·

1. Melt the marshmallows in the half-and-half in a double boiler. Remove the mixture from the heat and let it cool.

2. Fold in the crème de cacao and crème de menthe.

3. Whip the ½ pint cream and mix it into the filling mixture.

4. Pour the filling into the chilled crust.

5. Place the pie in the refrigerator and let it set for at least one hour.

6. Before serving, whip 4 tablespoons (60 grams) whipping cream and spread it over the top of the pie.

7. Sprinkle the cookie crumbs evenly over the top of the whipped cream. Add a mint sprig or two for garnish.

Angel Food Pie

Sue attended one of my pie workshops and we have stayed in touch ever since, sharing pie tips and photos of the old roses we both grow in our cottage gardens. Her stepmom, Alberta, a Southern beauty and brilliant cook who played sax and clarinet in a vaudeville band before going on to Hollywood and working on the Shirley Temple films, made this sweet pie for Sue when she was young. Tint the topping with one to two drops of red food coloring until it turns light pink and it's perfect to serve at a little girls' tea party.

MAKES ONE 9-INCH DEEP-DISH PIE

INGREDIENTS
· · · · ·

1¼ cups (310 grams) hot water

2½ tablespoons (20 grams) cornstarch

1 scant cup (200 grams) sugar plus 2 tablespoons (24 grams) for whipping cream

4 egg whites

A pinch of salt

1½ teaspoons (6 grams) vanilla extract, divided

1 blind-baked pie crust (see page 98)

1 pint (500 grams) whipping cream

1–2 drops red food coloring (optional)

Shredded, sweetened coconut for sprinkling

CONTINUED

PROCEDURE

· · · · ·

1. Set the water to boil. In the top of a double boiler, mix the corn-starch and sugar with a fork, then moisten with ¼ cup (60 grams) cold water and stir to make a paste.

2. Add the boiling water and mix with a wire whisk until the mixture is smooth. If you don't have a whisk, a fork or a spoon will do. Cook 15 minutes, stirring very often, then remove from heat.

3. Beat the egg whites until they are very stiff and then add spoonfuls of the cornstarch–sugar mixture to the egg whites, beating after each addition. Add one pinch of salt and 1 teaspoon vanilla (save the rest for the whipping cream) and mix briefly. Set this aside to cool.

4. In a pre-baked pie shell, use a spatula to pour in the egg white–sugar mixture.

5. Beat the whipping cream until it is thick. Add the remaining sugar and vanilla and beat briefly to incorporate them. Add the optional food coloring and beat for a few seconds more.

6. Spread the whipping cream thickly over the egg white–sugar mixture.

7. Sprinkle the coconut over the top.

· · · · · · · · · · · · · · · · · · **NOTES** · · · · · · · · · · · · · · · · ·

If using unsweetened coconut, you may add sugar to taste to sweeten it up.

For a variation, use ⅛ teaspoon almond extract in place of vanilla.

· ·

Berry Tart with Vanilla Cream

Every area of the country has regional strawberry varieties. My favorite is named Shuksan, after the peak in the Cascade Mountains. I began growing this variety in the mid 1980s and within three years was harvesting hundreds of pounds of ripe sweet berries each June. Strawberries are lovely showcased on top of this tart, making it almost, but not quite, too pretty to eat. Try it with ripe blueberries, raspberries, blackberries, or a combination of them all. For a different flavor, try replacing the vanilla with almond, rum, coconut, or orange extracts. Add sparingly and taste. I make this with lite coconut milk but you can use whole milk, or half-and-half if you are feeling exceptionally decadent.

MAKES ONE 9-INCH SHALLOW PIE OR TART

INGREDIENTS
· · · · ·

1 recipe Vanilla Pastry Cream (recipe follows)

1 blind-baked pie crust (see page 98)

1 pint fresh whole strawberries or other ripe berries

PROCEDURE
· · · · ·

1. Make the Vanilla Pastry Cream and chill it in the refrigerator.
2. When the cream is completely chilled, whisk lightly with a fork. Using a spatula, turn it into the baked crust and spread evenly.
3. Arrange the fruit in a pretty pattern on top.
4. Serve and enjoy!

CONTINUED

Vanilla Pastry Cream

INGREDIENTS

· · · · ·

4 egg yolks

1 tablespoon (12 grams) vanilla extract

¾ cup (150 grams) sugar

¼ cup (30 grams) cornstarch

1 (14-ounce) can (400 grams) lite coconut milk or 2 cups (500 grams) whole milk or half-and-half

PROCEDURE

· · · · ·

1. Place the egg yolks in a medium bowl. Add the vanilla extract and whisk into the yolks for a minute or so until the eggs are smooth. It's fine to do this with a fork. Set aside.

2. Place the sugar and cornstarch in a medium saucepan and mix together with a whisk or fork.

3. With a whisk in hand, turn the heat to medium under the saucepan, and pour the milk slowly and steadily into the dry ingredients while whisking constantly. Keep whisking until the mixture thickens and you see it begin to bubble.

4. Remove the pan from the heat momentarily and pour ⅓ of the hot mixture into the eggs in the bowl. Whisk together in the bowl until it looks blended in. This won't take long.

5. Pour the now hot egg mixture from the bowl into the saucepan and return it to the stovetop. Turn the heat back to medium, and whisk the mixture constantly until you bring it to a boil. It will be thick and coat the back of a spoon. Remove it from the heat.

6. Turn the hot mixture into a bowl and cover with parchment paper to prevent a skin from forming as it cools. Chill the mixture in the fridge for at least 2 hours.

Banana Rum Caramel Coconut Pie

This pie hits all of the pleasure points. It's sweet, creamy, has salted caramel and rum, and is a real showstopper. There are a number of elements to make, but once you have them ready, it's a snap to put together.

MAKES ONE 9-INCH DEEP-DISH PIE

INGREDIENTS
· · · · ·

4 bananas

1 blind-baked pie crust or a cookie crumb crust (see pages 94–98)

¼ cup (60 grams) Salted Rum Caramel Sauce (recipe follows, or use store-bought salted caramel sauce, plus more for optional drizzling)

1 recipe Rum Pastry Cream (recipe follows)

¼ cup (15 grams) toasted coconut chips

Whipping cream

PROCEDURE
· · · · ·

1. Peel the bananas and fit them tightly into the bottom of the pie shell.
2. Pour the Salted Rum Caramel Sauce over the bananas.
3. Lightly whisk the Rum Pastry Cream and, using a spatula, spread it evenly over the bananas and caramel.
4. Sprinkle toasted coconut pieces over top.
5. Before serving, drizzle the pie with caramel (optional) and place a dollop of whipped cream on each slice.

CONTINUED

Rum Pastry Cream

INGREDIENTS
· · · · ·

4 egg yolks

⅛ teaspoon (.5 gram) salt, plus a pinch

¾ cup (150 grams) sugar

¼ cup (30 grams) cornstarch

One 14-ounce (400 grams) can lite coconut milk, about 2 cups

¼ cup (60 grams) dark rum

1–2 teaspoons (4–8 grams) coconut extract (optional)

PROCEDURE
· · · · ·

1. Place the egg yolks in a medium bowl with a small pinch of salt. Whisk the yolks for a minute or so until they are smooth. It's fine to do this with a fork. Set the mixture aside.

2. Place the salt, sugar, and cornstarch in a medium saucepan, and mix together with a whisk.

3. Mix the coconut milk and rum together.

4. With a whisk in hand, turn the heat to medium under the saucepan and slowly and steadily pour the coconut rum milk into the dry ingredients while whisking constantly. Keep whisking until the mixture thickens and you see it begin to bubble.

5. Remove the mixture from the heat momentarily, and pour ⅓ of the hot mixture into the eggs in the bowl. Whisk together in the bowl until it looks blended in. This will temper the eggs and won't take long.

6. Pour the egg mixture back into the saucepan, and return it to the stovetop.

7. Turn the heat back to medium, and whisk the mixture constantly until you bring it to a boil. It will be thick and coat the back of a spoon. Remove it from the heat.

8. Using a spatula, turn the hot mixture into a bowl, and cover with parchment paper or plastic wrap to prevent a skin from forming as it cools. Cool completely in the refrigerator for at least 2 hours or overnight.

Salted Rum Caramel Sauce

INGREDIENTS

. . . . .

1 cup (200 grams) sugar

¼ cup (60 grams) water

½ teaspoon (3 grams) salt

½ cup (120 grams) whipping cream

¼ cup (60 grams) dark rum

PROCEDURE

. . . . .

1. In a medium saucepan, add the sugar and water. Turn the heat to high, whisk until the sugar dissolves, and bring to a boil.

2. Let the mixture boil until it turns a rich caramel color. This takes between 5 to 7 minutes. Swirl the pan slightly every once in a while.

3. Turn the heat to low and then add the salt, whipping cream, and rum. The mixture will bubble up with the additions so you will need to take care and stand back when adding.

4. Whisk again until all is smooth. Let the sauce boil for about 1 minute more.

5. Transfer the sauce to a glass jar or bowl to cool. Store extra caramel sauce in the refrigerator.

Mocha Cream Pie

I use strong dark Italian instant espresso to make a filling with rich mocha flavor. For a chocolate cream pie variation, leave the espresso out. Top it off with whipped cream (flavored with liqueur if desired) and serve with a few ripe raspberries. It is good with a cookie crumb crust or a standard pie crust, too.

MAKES ONE 9-INCH SHALLOW PIE

INGREDIENTS
. . . . .

1 recipe Gluten-Free Nutty No-Bake Crust (see page 92)

¾ cup (150 grams) sugar

1 tablespoon (5 grams) cocoa powder

1 tablespoon (5 grams) Italian instant espresso powder

¼ cup (30 grams) cornstarch

1 tablespoon (8 grams) flour

¼ teaspoon (1 gram) salt

2½ cups (600 grams) half-and-half, milk, or lite coconut milk
   (a mixture is fine, too)

1 teaspoon (4 grams) vanilla extract

4 large egg yolks

2 ounces (48 grams) unsweetened chocolate

2 tablespoons (14 grams) butter, salted or unsalted

Whipped cream, for topping

PROCEDURE

· · · · ·

1. Press the crust into a 9-inch shallow pie pan and chill.
2. In a 2-quart saucepan, combine the sugar, cocoa powder, instant espresso, cornstarch, flour, and salt.
3. Whisk in ½ cup half-and-half or whatever milk you are using, and mix until the mixture is smooth. Whisk in the remaining 2 cups of half-and-half or milk, add the vanilla and egg yolks, and whisk again. There should be no lumps.
4. Place the saucepan over medium high heat and whisk constantly until the mixture thickens and bubbles. Cook for two minutes more and remove from the heat.
5. Add the unsweetened chocolate pieces and butter and let sit for a few minutes to melt. Stir to blend.
6. Turn the hot mixture into a bowl and cover with parchment paper to prevent a skin from forming. Place in the mixture in the refrigerator for two to four hours, until the filling is completely cool.
7. Pour the chilled mocha cream into the chilled pie shell and spread evenly with a spatula.
8. Using a spatula, spread whipped cream on top of the mocha cream, or place a dollop on each slice when you serve.

VARIATIONS

· · · · ·

FLAVORED WHIPPED CREAM Try whipping 1 cup (240 grams) heavy cream with 2 tablespoons (24 grams) sugar and 2 tablespoons (30 grams) chocolate, coffee, or orange liqueur in place of plain whipped cream.

Chai Pie

During cooler weather I often have a big pot of homemade chai simmering on top of my woodstove. I learned a lot about the chai culture from Jenny and Patrick Shaw's book, *Chai Pilgrimage*, including how much better chai is when preparing spices in a spice grinder or a mortar and pestle just before they are to be used. I wondered if this might transfer to a pie, and this recipe is what I came up with. The flavors are subtle and not as sweet as what you might drink at the espresso stand.

MAKES ONE 9-INCH SHALLOW PIE

INGREDIENTS

· · · · ·

2½ cups (618 grams) lite coconut milk

20 cardamom pods, ground or crushed

½ teaspoon (1 gram) cinnamon, ground

1¼ teaspoons (3 grams) fennel seed, ground or crushed

1 tablespoon (5 grams) fresh ginger, peeled and grated

A few saffron threads

5–6 whole black peppercorns

4 whole allspice, lightly crushed

2 tea bags of black tea

1¼ cups (250 grams) sugar

⅓ cup (40 grams) cornstarch

¼ teaspoon (a pinch) salt

4 large eggs

2 tablespoons (30 grams) coconut oil or butter

1 blind-baked pie crust (see page 98)

Whipped cream, for topping

PROCEDURE

· · · · ·

1. Pour the coconut milk into a saucepan with the cardamom, cinnamon, fennel, ginger, saffron, peppercorns, and allspice. Bring to a simmer at about 185°F degrees (85°C) for about 10 minutes.

2. Add the tea bags, cover, and continue at a low simmer for 10 more minutes.

3. Remove the pan from the heat and pour the mixture through a strainer. Discard the solids and put the mixture back into the saucepan.

4. In a medium bowl combine the sugar, cornstarch, salt, and eggs. Add this mixture to the coconut spice tea mixture in the saucepan, and while whisking constantly, cook over a medium heat until the mixture thickens. This will take about 7 to 10 minutes.

5. Remove from heat and immediately add 2 tablespoons coconut oil or butter. Stir until the fats have melted.

6. Pour the mixture into a bowl. Place a piece of parchment paper on top of the custard so it will not form a skin. Place it in the fridge and chill for 2 to 3 hours.

7. When it's completely cool, remove the parchment and scrape off any custard that sticks to it. Using a spatula, pour or spoon the chilled custard into the already baked and waiting pie crust, and spread it out evenly.

8. Top with whipping cream or whipped coconut cream.

Chess Pie

There are a few different tales of how this well-known southern pie got its name. One is that it could be stored without refrigeration in a pie chest, or "chess." Another is that this simple custard pie is just pie, with "just" pronounced something close to "jes," or chess. My version is not as sweet as the traditional recipes I have seen, and I use flour instead of cornmeal in the filling. Many who have sampled a slice say they would eat this pie every day if they could.

MAKES ONE 9-INCH DEEP-DISH PIE

INGREDIENTS
· · · · ·

1 recipe single-crust pie dough

1½ cups (300 grams) sugar

6 tablespoons (54 grams) flour

¾ cup (168 grams) butter, softened

5 large eggs

1½ teaspoons (6 grams) vanilla extract

⅜ teaspoon (.75 gram) almond extract

1½ cups (375 grams) lite coconut milk or goat milk yogurt

PROCEDURE
· · · · ·

1. Preheat the oven to 425°F (220°C).
2. Roll out the pie dough and place it in a pie pan.
3. In a food processor, insert the steel blade. Add the sugar, flour, and butter, and mix until the batter is smooth.
4. Add the eggs, vanilla and almond extracts, and milk, and blend thoroughly.

5. Pour the filling into the pie shell and bake for 10 minutes at 425°F (220°C). After 10 minutes, reduce the heat to 350°F (175°C) and continue cooking 40 to 50 minutes.
6. When the pie is done, the crust will be set, and the filling shouldn't quiver when you gently shake the pie pan. The top will be golden.
7. Set the pie on a cooling rack for two hours. It will continue to set up.

· · · · · · · · · · · · · · · · · · · **NOTES** · · · · · · · · · · · · · · · ·

If you are gluten-free, use a gluten-free dough, and substitute Gluten-Free Flour Mix (page 79) for the flour in the filling. Another option for flavor is 1 teaspoon each vanilla and rum extracts. If you want to be totally spirited, add ¼ cup good sour mash bourbon.

· ·

VARIATIONS
· · · · ·

CHOCOLATE CHESS PIE Add ½ cup melted semi-sweet chocolate pieces. When you cut into the pie you will see both chocolate and custard layers.

BUTTERMILK PIE A variation on Chess Pie made with buttermilk. Use 1½ cups (375 grams) buttermilk instead of coconut milk.

Pecan Pie

My neighbor, Omma, was kind enough to share the pecan pie recipe her Aunt Agnes gave her. Aunt Agnes was born and raised in the South and remembered using freshly gathered pecans from trees in the woods surrounding their old farmhouse for this pie. Omma recalls that sometimes it was sweetened with wild honey sugared on top of their smokehouse. Serve slices with a dollop of sweetened whipped cream flavored with Kentucky bourbon or dark rum. À la mode with a scoop of French vanilla ice cream is also nice, and a sliver of pecan pie is always great for a midnight snack.

MAKES ONE 9-INCH SHALLOW PIE

INGREDIENTS
· · · · ·

1 recipe single-crust pie dough

3 large eggs

1 cup (220 grams) dark brown sugar, packed

½ cup (118 grams) dark corn syrup or pure maple syrup, or a combination of both

¼ teaspoon (a pinch) salt

1 teaspoon (4 grams) vanilla extract

4 tablespoons (60 grams) Kentucky bourbon, dark rum, or 1 tablespoon (15 grams) rum flavoring

¼ cup (56 grams) salted butter, melted

At least 2 cups (240 grams) shelled pecans, broken or chopped into pieces

1. Preheat the oven to 375°F (190°C).
2. Roll out a pie shell and place it in a pie pan. Trim excess dough from the edges and crimp.
3. Whisk the eggs in a medium bowl until they are light-colored and fluffy. Add the brown sugar, syrup, salt, vanilla, and bourbon or rum. Stir with big wooden spoon until the sugar is dissolved and the ingredients are thoroughly mixed.
4. Stir in the melted butter and pecans.
5. Pour the mixture into the pie shell and garnish with pecan halves. Bake on a middle oven rack for 45 to 50 minutes, and there is a slight jiggle in the center of the pie. Cool the pie on a wire rack.

· · · · · · · · · · · · · · · · · · · **NOTES** · · · · · · · · · · · · · · · · ·

Buy the freshest nuts you can find. Reserve some of the nicest-looking unbroken halves for garnish. Watch to make sure the pecans don't overly brown during the bake.

· ·

VARIATION
· · · · ·

CHOCOLATE PECAN PIE Melt ½ cup (95 grams) semi-sweet chocolate pieces and fold them into the filling before baking.

Pumpkin Pie

This pie should have a slight jiggle in the middle, about the size of a silver dollar, when it comes out of the oven. It will "set up" as it cools.

MAKES ONE 9-INCH SHALLOW PIE

INGREDIENTS

· · · · ·

1 recipe single-crust pie dough

3 eggs, lightly beaten

One 15-ounce can (about 2 cups or 425 grams) pumpkin

1 cup canned lite coconut milk or evaporated milk

¾ cup (150 grams) sugar (equal parts white and packed brown sugar)

½ teaspoon (3 grams) salt

1 teaspoon (2 grams) cinnamon

1 teaspoon (2 grams) ginger

¼ teaspoon (.25 gram) freshly ground nutmeg

A tiny pinch of ground clove

PROCEDURE

· · · · ·

1. Preheat the oven to 425°F (220°C).
2. Roll out a pie shell and place it in a pie pan. Trim excess dough from the edges and crimp.
3. Whisk the eggs in a medium bowl until they are light-colored and fluffy. Stir in the pumpkin, coconut milk, sugar, salt, cinnamon, ginger, nutmeg, and clove until the ingredients are thoroughly mixed.
4. Pour the filling into the pan. Place the pie in the oven and turn down immediately to 375°F. Bake for approximately 50 minutes.
5. Remove the pie from the oven and set on a rack to cool completely.

CHAPTER EIGHT

Savory Supper Pies

There's just no way around the fact that parenting
during the teenage years is challenging. I became sullen and silent, and my son was no different. My mom and I walked together to connect, but it was the regularity of home-cooked meals on the table that worked for Duncan and me. Full breakfasts every morning, lunches packed in brown paper bags through all of his high school years, and after I finished teaching the day's piano lessons, a simple supper that included homemade soups, pizza, and pies both savory and sweet.

Even with the hope of a scholarship to college, when Duncan was in high school, it became pretty evident that I would need a way to supplement my income as a musician to make ends meet and give my boy the chance of a higher education. Opportunity always knocks when truly needed and this time it came in the form of an offer to stuff envelopes for Taylor Shellfish Farms. It was the bottom rung of the ladder but I was grateful for a way to fill the college coffers. I could do the work at home in my off hours from teaching and many times in a bathrobe and slippers. As the years went by, I was given more and more responsibilities and worked my way up with the company. I didn't know that much about shellfish when I began, but with plentiful opportunities to sample and cook oysters, mussels, and clams, I learned. Clams became a house favorite and Duncan, continuing to show ease in the kitchen, learned that it took only a few minutes at night to cook up a pan full of Manilas and impress his friends with some quick homemade food. The biggest surprise may have

been when I made a delicious savory pie with one of Taylor's geoduck clams. Since then it's become a family favorite and one we delight in sharing with others who join us at our table.

Pies have been around for a very long time and there is simply no limit to what they can be filled with. Just about every culture that baked bread also used dough as a carrier for filling. In *The Canterbury Tales*, Chaucer writes of the pie dealer who was known for selling pasties "that hath been twies hoot and twies coold," not fresh as one would hope. In medieval times, a pie's tough and sturdy shell, called a coffin, was a far cry from the tender and flaky crusts we enjoy today. Firm walls that were inches thick took several hours to bake and were considered inedible, at least by those who sat at the head of the table and savored the meat filling baked inside. The lower the position one had at the table, the more of the coffin on the plate. The remaining portions went to the scullery and the last scraps to those who begged outside the lord and lady's gate. Having no way to preserve food, the coffin was a way to seal and bake food that could be taken on the road. I think of it as the original Tupperware. It was sometimes refilled with a new filling, and could be reused as thickener for other dishes, too. As much as that makes me feel a bit squeamish, a mention in *The Oxford Companion to Sugar and Sweets* floored me when I read of a 1695 recipe for boar pie that says "if sealed with butter, 'if it be not set in a very moist place, keep a whole Year.' " A whole year? Yes, it certainly was a different time. Today we enjoy tender versions of versatile, savory pies with a purpose that remains the same: a nourishing meal to come home to.

· · · · · · · · · · · · · · · · **PIE SUPPERS** · · · · · · · · · · · · · · · ·

Pie suppers of earlier days featured pies that were auctioned off to raise money in rural areas, usually for a specific need such as books for the library or supplies for the school. The winning bidder then had the privilege of sharing the pie with its baker, often a young or single woman. It's been said that many a courtship was cemented over pie.

· ·

Chicken Pot Pie

A favorite childhood memory is eating chicken pot pie at Manning's Copper Coffee Pot in Santa Barbara with my grandmother. Thick golden crusts full of butter were cut in squares and draped over the edges of single-serving, deep-dish, oven-proof bowls. This set the standard for what I believe a good pot pie should be. I make individual pies for my family and big pot pies for gatherings with friends.

MAKES ONE 9-INCH DEEP-DISH POT PIE OR FOUR 5½-INCH MINI POT PIES

INGREDIENTS
· · · · ·

1 recipe double-crust pie dough, if you're making your pie with both top and bottom crust (use 1 recipe single-crust pie dough for top crust only)

About 1½ pounds (680 grams) chicken thighs

3 tablespoons (45 grams) olive oil

1 large onion, peeled and chopped small

3 stalks celery, sliced into ¼-inch (.6 centimeter) moons

3 red potatoes, cut into ½-inch (1 centimeter) pieces

½ teaspoon dry thyme, or leaves from 6–8 fresh sprigs

2 large carrots, peeled and sliced into ¼-inch moons

½ cup (73 grams) flour

1 teaspoon (4 grams) sugar

1 teaspoon (6 grams) salt

¼ teaspoon (a pinch) freshly ground black pepper

1 cup (150 grams) frozen peas, unthawed

2 tablespoons (30 grams) dry sherry (optional)

EGG WASH

1 egg mixed with 2 tablespoons (30 grams) water

CONTINUED

PROCEDURE

· · · · ·

1. Prepare and chill the dough.

2. In a large pot, cover the chicken thighs with water and bring them to a boil. Lower the heat to simmer and cover the pot. Simmer for 10 minutes, then turn off the heat and let the pot sit, covered, for one hour.

3. In the meantime, heat the olive oil in a large frying pan or saucepan. Add the onion, celery, potatoes, and thyme. Cook over medium-low heat until they are soft, about 20 minutes.

4. When the chicken is ready, remove the chicken and reserve the stock. Allow it to cool. Pull apart or cut the meat into small pieces, then cover it and place it in the fridge.

5. In a saucepan, put 4 cups (908 grams) of the chicken stock and boil for about 5 minutes. Add carrots and cook for 10 minutes more, then remove the pan from the heat.

6. Remove the carrots and set them aside. Reserve the stock for the filling.

7. Add the flour, sugar, salt, and pepper to the onions, celery, and potatoes; stir, and cook over low heat for 2 minutes. Stir in the stock a little at a time.

8. Turn heat up and then simmer for 10 minutes, stirring occasionally, until it looks like a thick soup; then remove from the heat.

9. Stir in the peas, optional dry sherry, chicken, and carrots, and salt and pepper to taste. Cool for 15 to 20 minutes while you preheat the oven to 425°F (220°C).

10. Pour the filling into a deep-dish pie pan or spoon it into individual pie pans.

11. Top with the rolled out dough and cut some vents on top.

12. Brush the pie with egg wash.

13. Bake for about 30 minutes.

· · · · · · · · · · · · · DOUBLE-CRUST PIE · · · · · · · · · · ·

You can make this pie with a bottom crust, too. Roll out the bottom crust and place it in the pan before putting the filling in. Trim and crimp the edges. Place it on a preheated cookie sheet when baking for the bottom crust to bake up.

· ·

VARIATIONS
· · · · ·

PARMESAN-CHICKEN PIE Add 1 cup grated Parmesan cheese.

CHEDDAR-CHICKEN PIE Top with a Cheddar Cheese Crust (see page 63 or, for a gluten-free crust, 86).

Cottage Pie

I look forward to the quieter time of the year, when friends stop by to spend an afternoon with knitting needles and threads of conversation by my woodstove. My cottage smells like the savory taste of fall when I bake this satisfying comfort food to share.

MAKES ONE LARGE PIE

INGREDIENTS
· · · · ·

1½ pounds (about 700 grams) ground beef

2½ teaspoons thyme (dry is just fine—or 1 tablespoon fresh leaves, finely chopped), divided

¼ teaspoon allspice

2 gratings nutmeg

1 teaspoon (6 grams) salt

⅓ teaspoon (1 gram) freshly ground black pepper

2 medium yellow onions, peeled and chopped small

5 cloves garlic, peeled and diced

2 large carrots, grated

2½ tablespoons (about 40 grams) tomato paste

1 cup (227 grams) stock (vegetable, beef, or chicken)

2¼ pounds (1 kilogram) potatoes, peeled and cut in quarters

⅓ cup (75 grams) butter

1 cup (200 grams) cheddar cheese, grated and divided

Salt and pepper

PROCEDURE

· · · · ·

1. Heat up a big frying pan over medium high heat. Add the meat and seasonings (reserve ½ teaspoon of thyme), and cook until the meat no longer looks pink. You can break the larger piece up a bit as you are cooking it.

2. Add the vegetables and cook for 5 to 7 minutes longer.

3. Stir in the tomato paste and cook for a few minutes more.

4. Add the stock, reduce the heat, and simmer uncovered for 15 to 20 minutes.

5. In another pot, cover the potatoes with water plus 1 teaspoon (6 grams) of salt and boil until they are tender, about 20 minutes. Drain well and put them back into the pot with the butter, ⅔ cup of the cheese, and remaining ½ teaspoon thyme.

6. Mash the potatoes until they are smooth. Add salt and pepper to your taste.

7. Spoon the meat mixture into a deep-dish pie pan or a large baking dish.

8. Cover with the potato mixture and sprinkle the remaining ⅓ cup cheese over the top.

9. When ready to bake, preheat oven to 425°F (220°C) and bake for 35 minutes.

Shepherd's Pie

A shepherd's pie is made with lamb and topped with mashed potatoes. I add a cup of grated sharp cheddar cheese to the potatoes along with some dried thyme harvested from my herb garden in the summer, which I dry for use all year long.

MAKES ONE LARGE PIE

INGREDIENTS
. . . . .

1½ pounds (about 700 grams) ground lamb

2½ teaspoons thyme (dry is just fine—or 1 tablespoon fresh leaves), divided

¼ teaspoon allspice

2 gratings nutmeg

1 teaspoon (6 grams) salt

⅓ teaspoon (1 gram) freshly ground black pepper

2 medium yellow onions, peeled and chopped small

5 cloves garlic, peeled and diced

2 large carrots, grated

2½ tablespoons (about 40 grams) tomato paste

1 cup (227 grams) stock, vegetable, beef, or chicken

2¼ pounds (1 kilogram) potatoes, peeled and cut in quarters

⅓ cup (75 grams) butter

1 cup (200 grams) cheddar cheese, grated and divided

Salt and pepper

CONTINUED

PROCEDURE

·　·　·　·　·

1. Heat up a big frying pan over medium high heat. Add the meat and seasonings (reserve ½ teaspoon of thyme), and cook until the meat no longer looks pink. You can break the larger piece up a bit as you are cooking it.

2. Add the vegetables and cook for 5 to 7 minutes longer.

3. Stir in the tomato paste, and cook for a few minutes more.

4. Add the stock, reduce the heat, and simmer uncovered for 15 to 20 minutes.

5. In another pot, cover the potatoes with water plus 1 teaspoon (6 grams) of salt and boil until they are tender, about 20 minutes. Drain well and put them back into the pot with the butter, ⅔ cup cheese, and remaining ½ teaspoon thyme.

6. Mash the potatoes until they are smooth. Add salt and pepper to your taste.

7. Spoon the meat mixture into a deep-dish pie pan or a large baking dish.

8. Cover with the potato mixture and sprinkle the remaining ⅓ cup of cheese over the top.

9. When ready to bake, preheat oven to 425°F (220°C) and bake for 35 minutes.

Sausage and Apple Pie

It was quite something to experience an entire photo shoot come to a halt when this richly scented savory pie emerged from the oven. After the last shot was taken, a green salad and bottle of white wine quickly materialized, but by the time I got to the makeshift table for a piece, the pie had all but disappeared.

MAKES ONE 9-INCH DEEP-DISH PIE

INGREDIENTS

· · · · ·

1 recipe double Cheddar Cheese Crust (page 63 or, for a gluten-free crust, 86)

1 pound (454 grams) ground pork sausage, cooked and drained

2–3 tart apples (such as Granny Smiths) cored and sliced or roughly chopped

2–3 sweet apples, cored and sliced or roughly chopped

¼ teaspoon (a pinch) salt

1 cup (248 grams) apple juice or cider

⅓ cup (73 grams) brown sugar, packed

½ teaspoon dried thyme

¼ teaspoon fresh diced rosemary

¼ teaspoon allspice

EGG WASH

1 egg plus 2 tablespoons (30 grams) water, fork beaten

CONTINUED

PROCEDURE

· · · · ·

1. Cook the sausage and set it aside.

2. Place the apples, salt, juice or cider, brown sugar, thyme, rosemary, and allspice in a sauté or fry pan and cook on medium-low heat until you can just start to put a fork into the apples. Remove the pan from the heat and set it aside. Reserve the juice.

3. Pour the juice into a small saucepan. If you have less than a cup, add more juice or cider to make 1 cup, then turn the heat to low and cook until the juice has reduced in amount to about one quarter its amount and has nearly caramelized. Be careful not to let it burn. This will take about 10 to 12 minutes.

4. Spoon the sausage into the apple mixture, pour over the reduced cider, and mix well.

5. Adjust the salt to taste and let the filling cool.

6. Preheat the oven to 400°F (205°C). Roll out the bottom crust and place in your pie pan. Add the filling.

7. Roll out the upper crust and place it on top. Seal the edges, crimp, and vent.

8. Brush the pie with egg wash.

9. Bake for 40 minutes. Give the pie two more egg washes at 10-minute intervals during the first 20 minutes of the bake.

10. Let the pie cool for 15 minutes or more before serving.

· · · · · · · · · · · · · · · · · · **NOTES** · · · · · · · · · · · · · · · · · · ·

This pie can be made with or without a bottom crust. Depending on the type of apples used, there may be a lot of moisture in the filling and the bottom crust will soak it up.

It is delicious with a gluten-free cheddar crust, too. The cheddar cheese crust is a little sturdier than a crust without cheese, so don't make the edges too thick.

· ·

Savory Summer Harvest Ratatouille Pie

I was invited to teach at an olive oil ranch in central California where I put together a filling using the cornucopia of ripe and ready vegetables from the farm garden. According to what is available at my own farmers' market, the specific ingredients change every time I make this pie, so feel free to improvise and embellish with what is in season at yours.

MAKES ONE 9-INCH DEEP-DISH PIE

INGREDIENTS
. . . . .

½ cup (118 grams) organic virgin olive oil

1 medium to large onion, chopped

2 cloves garlic (more if you like)

1 eggplant, peeled and cubed

2 medium zucchini, cubed

1 sweet pepper, seeded and chopped

4 tomatoes, peeled, seeded, and cubed

2 teaspoons (10 grams) red wine vinegar

1 recipe double-crust pie dough

1 handful of fresh basil, chopped

Salt and pepper to taste

EGG WASH

1 egg plus 2 tablespoons (30 grams) water, fork beaten

CONTINUED

PROCEDURE

· · · · ·

1. In a heavy frying pan, heat the olive oil over medium heat.
2. Add the onion and garlic and cook until the onions are wilted (about 8 to 10 minutes).
3. Add the eggplant and cook for another 5 minutes.
4. Add the zucchini, pepper, tomatoes, and vinegar, cover, and cook for about 30 minutes, until the vegetables have cooked down a bit. If there is too much liquid, remove the cover and reduce.
5. Stir in the chopped basil and cool the filling completely. If there is still a lot of liquid in the pan, place the filling in a mesh colander and let the juice drip through. Add salt and pepper to taste.
6. Roll out one disc of pie dough and place it in a pie pan.
7. Pour the cooled filling into the unbaked pie shell and top with a lattice crust, or a full top crust with vents.
8. Chill the pie while you are preheating the oven to 475°F (246°C).
9. Brush the pie with egg wash.
10. Bake for 10 minutes.
11. Turn the oven down to 375°F (190°C) and bake for 20 minutes more, or until the crust is a nice golden color.

Italian Nettle Sausage Pie

Forager and author Langdon Cook and I created this pie together one afternoon with a bagful of fresh nettles he had gathered. Nettles grow in the rich soil of partially shaded areas throughout most of the world. They do sting, so wear gloves and long sleeves when you harvest them. When they are blanched the sting is neutralized. Replace the nettles with spinach for tasty results in this hearty supper pie.

FOR ONE 9–10-INCH DEEP-DISH PIE

INGREDIENTS
· · · · ·

1 pound (453 grams) sweet Italian sausage

3 leeks, thinly sliced (discard green tops)

4 large cloves garlic, chopped

6 eggs, reserving one for the egg wash

20 ounces (567 grams) stinging nettles, blanched and squeezed dry

4 cups (344 grams) shredded mozzarella cheese

1 cup (248 grams) ricotta cheese

1 teaspoon (6 grams) salt

¼ teaspoon (a pinch) freshly ground black pepper

A few gratings of fresh nutmeg

⅛ teaspoon red pepper flakes

2 teaspoons (10 grams) freshly squeezed lemon juice

1 recipe double-crust pie dough

EGG WASH

1 egg yolk plus 2 tablespoons (30 grams) water, fork beaten

PROCEDURE

· · · · ·

1. In a skillet over medium heat, sauté the sausage, leeks, and garlic.

2. Separate one egg and set the yolk aside to be used later for the egg wash. In a mixing bowl, beat the egg white and remaining eggs.

3. Mix in the nettles, mozzarella cheese, ricotta cheese, salt, pepper, nutmeg, red pepper flakes, lemon juice, and sausage mixture.

4. Line a deep 9- or 10-inch pie dish with pie dough (with a 9-inch dish you will likely have leftover filling).

5. Add the filling. Cover the pie with the top dough. Trim, seal, and flute the edges. Cut 6 vents in the top. Chill the pie while you are preheating the oven to 425°F (220°C).

6. Brush the pie with egg yolk wash.

7. Bake the pie for 20 minutes, then lower heat to 400°F (204°C) for another 30 minutes or until crust is golden brown and the filling is bubbly. Let the pie stand for 10 minutes before cutting.

You Pick the Seasoning Meat Pie

With this pie, you will be mixing up some good quality ground beef with spices, placing it between a full crust, and baking it. You might think of it as a meat loaf inside a crust. I'll give you some suggestions for seasoning, but it's fine to try others. This is another pie to serve family on a cold winter's night or share at a potluck.

MAKES ONE PIE

INGREDIENTS
· · · · ·

1½ pounds (700 grams) ground beef

1 large onion, minced

4 cloves garlic, minced

1 recipe double-crust pie dough

SEASONING OPTION 1: ITALIAN

1 teaspoon dried basil

1 teaspoon dried oregano

½ teaspoon dried parsley

A pinch of freshly ground nutmeg

1 tablespoon (15 grams) tomato paste

1 teaspoon (6 grams) salt

½ teaspoon (1.25 grams) freshly ground black pepper

1½ teaspoons (4 grams) ground cumin

1–2 teaspoons (1–2 grams) chili powder

1 teaspoon (6 grams) salt

½ teaspoon (1 gram) pepper

1 (4-ounce) can diced green chilies (optional)

SEASONING OPTION 3: PARSLEY, SAGE, ROSEMARY, & THYME

½ teaspoon dried parsley

¼ teaspoon dried sage

¼ teaspoon dried rosemary

1 teaspoon dried thyme

1 teaspoon (6 grams) salt

½ teaspoon (1.25 grams) freshly ground black pepper

EGG WASH

1 egg plus 2 tablespoons (30 grams) water, fork beaten

PROCEDURE

· · · · ·

1. Place the meat, onions, garlic, and seasoning option of your choice in a bowl and stir to mix.
2. Roll out the bottom dough and place it in a pie pan.
3. Turn meat mixture into the pie pan.
4. Roll out the second dough and place it on top of meat filling.
5. Crimp the edges and refrigerate while you are preheating the oven to 500°F (246°C).
6. Brush the pie with egg wash.
7. Bake the pie for 15 minutes.
8. Turn the oven down to 350°F (177°C) and bake for an additional 40 minutes.

Traditional English Pork Pies

I learned the technique of making hand-formed English pork pies at the School of Artisan Food in Nottinghamshire from Sarah Pettegree, master pork pie maker. According to my English friends, a good pork pie absolutely must have "the jelly," which is made with chicken bouillon and gelatin.

MAKES 2 SMALL PIES

INGREDIENTS
· · · · ·

2 pounds (907 grams) boneless pork shoulder (ask the butcher to grind 1½ pounds [680 grams] coarse grind, and leave the remaining ½ pound [226 grams] for you to chop into very small pieces)

¼ pound (113 grams) uncured pork belly, chopped into small pieces

2 teaspoon (12 grams) salt

1 teaspoon (.7 gram) ground sage

¾ teaspoon (3 grams) white pepper

½–¾ teaspoon (about 3 grams) Worcestershire sauce

⅛ teaspoon nutmeg

1 recipe English Hot Water Pastry (page 65)

1 recipe Jelly (recipe follows)

EGG WASH

1 egg plus 2 tablespoons (30 grams) water, fork beaten

PREPARE THE FILLING
· · · · ·

1. Mix together the pork, pork belly, salt, sage, white pepper, Worcestershire sauce, and nutmeg in a big bowl using your clean hands.

CONTINUED

2. Cook a tablespoon of the meat mixture in a sauté or fry pan over medium heat until done (5 minutes or so). Let it cool a bit and taste it. This way you can adjust the seasonings as needed for the remainder of the meat mixture. Do not cook the rest of the meat, but cover and refrigerate for a few hours or overnight so the flavors can blend.

TO FORM THE PIES
· · · · ·

1. Lightly flour a flat surface and roll one dough ball out to approximately a 6-inch (15 centimeters) square.
2. Flour the bottom of a jar that is a bit smaller than the size of your finished pie. (I use either a canning jar or a 500-milliliter French water glass.)
3. Turn the jar upside down and drape the dough over it. With your fingers, press the dough against the sides of the jar, stretching and smoothing it until the glass is covered. It should be about ⅓ inch (1 centimeter) thick. Chill in the refrigerator for about 5 minutes.
4. Remove the dough from the refrigerator and carefully remove the formed dough from the jar.
5. Fill the dough completely and firmly with meat mixture, and trim off any extra dough.
6. Gather the extra dough, re-form into a ball, and roll to a shape and thickness to fit the lid of the pie.
7. Brush a little water around the edges of the dough, cover the pie, and press the edges together. Trim excess dough off and finish the edges.
8. With the scraps, form a small rose or leaves and place it on top of the pie.
9. With the handle of a wooden spoon, make a steam hole in the top crust.
10. Chill the pie for a minimum of an hour and then bake (baking instructions follow) or wrap in butcher wrap and freeze.

TO BAKE
· · · · ·

1. Preheat the oven to 425°F (220°C).
2. Place the pies on a foil- or parchment-lined sheet pan.

3. Using a pastry brush, brush the lid and lip of the pie with the egg wash.

4. Bake for two 10-minute periods, brushing with the egg wash each time.

5. Turn the oven down to 400°F (205°C) and bake for an additional 60 to 70 minutes.

6. Remove the pies from the oven but leave them on the pan. The internal temperature should be 176°F (80°C) or above.

· · · · · · · · · · · · · · · · · · **NOTE** · · · · · · · · · · · · · · · · · ·

For a frozen pie, do not defrost the pie but add an additional 20 to 30 minutes of baking time.

· ·

Jelly

Add the jelly after the pie has cooled at least 30 minutes or when it is completely cool.

INGREDIENTS
· · · · ·

1 chicken bouillon cube

1 cup (120 grams) water

1–1½ packets (7–10 grams) gelatin

PROCEDURE
· · · · ·

1. Put 1 chicken bouillon cube in boiling water and let it dissolve. Turn off the heat and add gelatin and mix well.

2. Insert the tip of a baster into the steam hole at the top of the pie, and slowly add as much juice as each pie will take.

3. Let the pies cool, covered, on the pan completely. Serve at room temperature.

Great Big Clam Deep-Dish Pie

Geoduck is a native Nisqually word that means "digs deep" and is pronounced "gwee-duck." I love this pie made with a gluten-free cheddar cheese crust (see page 86).

MAKES ONE 9–10-INCH DEEP-DISH PIE

INGREDIENTS
· · · · ·

1 geoduck clam weighing 1½–2 ½ pounds (675–1125 grams)

1 large onion, chopped

4 cloves garlic, finely chopped

2 stalks celery, chopped

1 handful Italian flat-leaf parsley, chopped

3 tablespoons (45 grams) good quality olive oil

8 pieces bacon

5 small to medium red potatoes, chopped

½ teaspoon sage

½ teaspoon rosemary

1 teaspoon thyme

1–2 tablespoons (15–30 grams) Mama Lil's Peppers or other pickled red peppers in oil, (optional)

Salt and pepper to taste

A few shavings of black truffle (optional)

1 recipe double-crust pie dough or 1 recipe double cheddar cheese crust (page 63)

EGG WASH

1 egg yolk plus 2 tablespoons (30 grams) water

PREPARE THE GEODUCK MEAT

. . . . .

1. Fill a big stock pot with water, cover, and bring to a rolling boil. With tongs, quickly submerge the entire geoduck, shell and all, into the boiling water for 10 seconds. Remove the geoduck from the pot with tongs and immediately submerge it in a bowl of ice water for a few seconds.

2. Remove the geoduck from the ice water. With a sharp knife, quickly make a cut along the inside of each shell half. Discard the shells.

3. Make an additional cut along the middle of the body (the mantle) and remove and discard everything inside.

4. Remove the siphon casing that covers the long neck of the geoduck and discard.

5. Rinse the body (the mantle) and neck (the siphon) well in very cold water.

6. Slice and chop (the mantle) and neck (the siphon) to about the size you would for small pieces of meat in a chicken pot pie.

MAKE THE FILLING

. . . . .

1. Chop the onion, garlic, celery, and parsley, and sauté them in olive oil over medium low heat until the onion is soft.

2. In another pan, cook the bacon over medium heat.

3. Drain the bacon on paper towels and then chop into 1-inch (2–3 centimeters) pieces. Add the bacon to the onion mixture.

4. Add the sage, rosemary, thyme, chopped geoduck pieces, and optional peppers. Cook slowly for a few minutes to blend the flavors.

5. Add salt and pepper to taste. The optional truffle shavings will be added to the top of the filling when it is in the pie pan.

6. Set the mixture aside to cool.

CONTINUED

CONSTRUCT THE PIE

· · · · ·

1. Roll out a pie dough and place it in a pie pan.

2. Pour in the cooled filling. Place the optional black truffle shavings over the top.

3. Roll out the top crust and place it over the filling. Trim and crimp the edges. Cut a few vents on top of the pie. Chill while you preheat the oven to 425°F (220°C).

4. Fork beat egg yolk and water together in small bowl and brush it over the top of the pie.

5. Place the pie on the center rack of the oven and bake for two 10-minute periods, brushing with the egg wash each time. Turn the oven down to 375°F (190°C) and bake for an additional 30 to 35 minutes until you see some steam coming out of the vents and the top of the pie is golden.

6. Cool for 10 to 15 minutes before serving.

WHAT I'VE LEARNED FROM PIE

Well my friends, here we are at the end of our journey and I hope you have found our time together to be as enjoyable for you as it has been for me. Writing this book has given me a wonderful opportunity to pass on to you many of the tips and tricks I've picked up over my years at the baking counter both as a pie maker and a pie teacher. I never imagined myself as a teacher. When I was in music school, I thought the teaching profession was for those who didn't have "chops." But over decades in the field, I have learned that not only does one have to have "chops," one must be able to explain the why and how of their craft in five, ten, even fifteen different ways. If none of these explanations work, a good teacher will come up with more ways until a student "gets" it. I've found that the more I practice my craft, the more I learn and have to share with others. There is always some new trick or fascinating piece of history that I tuck away to be called out and shared at just the right time. I don't believe that I could have planned a career quite as unique as teaching pie making. It provides ongoing learning, sharing, and joy, and it gives great meaning to my life.

During pie workshops, I find deep satisfaction helping participants at the baking counter. When the time comes to pick up the rolling pin, some are shaking in their boots, but inevitably I see them finish up with a new skill they want to continue to practice and share. As they see their finished pies come out of the oven, they are like new parents, overjoyed with what they have created. I have watched generations of family members enjoy an afternoon of memory-making as they roll out dough and make fillings together. I am honored to be witness to the hearts that are opened during workshops where sweet and sometimes especially poignant stories are shared.

Lynne wrote that when her mother-in-law returned to India after the class they took together, she had the wiring redone in her flat and an oven installed so she could make pies in Calcutta. Brendan dropped me a line to say that after losing his job and identity, "Pie class made me feel whole once again." At one workshop, I helped Kate, a young scientist who had lost speech and the use of one side of her body after a stroke, roll out dough and cut perfect lattice strips with a scientist's precision.

I teach because it is the hope of a future memory. Annie, who was pregnant with Ruby when she came to her first pie class, expresses this sentiment best in an email she sent me. "It's been five years since my life was changed by the afternoon I spent making pie magic with you. I felt the magic all over again this weekend with my little gal, Ruby, who loves to bake with me. On Sunday, she learned all about chubby discs and the sizzle-whump, and oodles of other wonderful things that helped make our nectarine blueberry pie taste like pure love. Thank you so much for that first special pie, and all the pies since, and all the pies to come!"

The craft of pie, both making and teaching, has been passed on to my beloved son, who can roll with the best of them. Duncan was helping me bake as soon as he could climb up on the baking counter as a toddler in the late 1980s,

and in 2015 won a coveted green-and-white "Best in Show" ribbon, receiving even higher marks than I did when I was awarded the same honor. To say that I am one proud pie mama would be a big understatement.

I receive emails from folks who, years after their workshops, continue to enjoy making pies. One email puts it all together. Rex decided to celebrate sixty years of life by making sixty pies, more than one each week, before his next birthday rolled around. Over that year he made "pies of celebration, pies of grief and all sorts of pies in between— each one with its own unique story to tell. They have offered the opportunity to enter into community and learning in ways I never would have thought possible. I can't tell you how many times I have looked out the window to see a pie plate returning home filled with something warm and gracious. And when asked 'how did you learn to do that?' I tell them about my pie mentor, Kate, and the remarkable experience that it was to sit in her presence and learn all about the gifts that come from making pie."

And the gift that I have learned from pie making? Well, that can be summed up in just one word . . . love.

Kate's Very Short Glossary of Pie-Making Terms

CHUBBY DISCS Round discs of dough similar in size to the buns of a famous space princess. Some also say they are about the size of hockey pucks.

MOOKIE-MESS What your dough will roll out like if pieces of ice are left to melt inside of it.

SIZZLE-WHUMP The sound a double-crust pie makes when it is ready to come out of the oven. The crust makes a sizzling sound and the bubbling filling will hit the inside of the upper crust making a whumping noise. Some folks say this is the sound of the pie's heartbeat.

SMOOSH A highly technical term for rubbing the cold fat into the cold flour with your cold hands when making dough by hand.

TCHOO-TCHOO-TCHOO The sound to make when removing plastic wrap from gluten-free dough with quick little tugs.

TCHOOOOOOOOOOOOO...OOPS The sound to make when removing plastic wrap from gluten-free dough with one fast, long pull.

PIE EATER One who enjoys pie for breakfast, lunch, dinner, dessert, and everything in between, including middle-of-the-night snacks. When the pie eater enters the kitchen, their roving eye scans every surface for possible booty. Pie eaters are known to raid refrigerators of family and friends, and even strangers without remorse. Pie eaters can always be counted on to finish up the last slice.

PIE MAKER One who makes and bakes home-made pies. A pie maker may hold this honored title and revered status in family lore for generations. The scepter of the pie maker is a well-seasoned rolling pin. The pie maker is the loving guardian of family recipes and practices them regularly. Any changes or additions are noted in the margins on well-worn and stained index cards, newspaper clippings, and recipe books. The pie maker is charged with passing the craft, rolling pin, and recipes on to the next generation.

PIE SEEKER One who is on the never-ending quest for the best pie. Upon hearing of a tender and flaky crust, exceptional filling, or light-as-air meringue, the pie seeker will automatically set a course to sample a slice. Pie seekers have made entire journeys across the United States searching for a perfect piece. Everyone needs a quest. What better one than pie?

PIE LOVE The moment a just-baked pie emerges from the oven and the baker only has eyes for it. Sometimes accompanied by words like "I can't believe I made this. It's the most beautiful pie ever!"

How to Render Leaf Lard

- Ask your butcher for "leaf lard—not back fat, please." Five to 6 pounds (2.25 to 2.75 kilograms) is a decent amount to make 4 or 5 pints worth. Look at it to make sure it doesn't have a lot, or preferably any red meat on it. If it has a lot, it may be back fat which is not as high quality.
- With a clean sharp knife, chop the fat into small pieces about the size of almonds.
- Cover the bottom of a heavyweight stockpot, Dutch oven, or fry pan with a bit of water. Spread the pieces of fat evenly over the surface of the pan.
- If you are rendering on a stovetop, turn the burner to low, and set the pot on top. In the oven, preheat to 250°F (120°C), and place the pot inside. Then relax and stir occasionally while the fat melts. The white fat will turn clear as it melts—think melting bacon fat here. Five to 6 pounds (2.25 to 2.75 kilograms) of fat can take three hours or so in the oven, but less time on the stovetop.
- Be sure that the fat doesn't scorch or it will give a give a noticeable flavor to the finished leaf lard.
- When most of the pieces are melted, carefully pour the clear hot fat through a double layer of cheesecloth and into a bowl. Ladle out any remaining fat bits and finish by ladling into jars. Let cool completely before you put on the lids.
- Optionally, you can let the rendered leaf lard cool completely in the bowl, weigh out 4-ounce (112 grams) pieces, individually wrap, and freeze in dated freezer bags. When you feel a pie making session coming on, you're already one step ahead.

The porcine aroma of rendering is likely one you are unfamiliar with. Rendering may have taken place out of doors in a manner similar to the directions in *The White House Cookbook* from 1898 if your great-great grandparents lived on a farm.

"Skin the leaf lard carefully, cut it into small pieces and put it into a kettle or saucepan; pour in a cupful of water to prevent burning; set it over the fire where it will melt slowly. Stir it frequently and let it simmer until nothing remains but brown scraps. Remove the scraps with a perforated skimmer, stir in a little salt to settle the fat, and, when clear, strain through a coarse cloth into jars . . . If it scorches, it gives it a bad flavor."

Other uses for lard? It makes fabulous tasting tortilla chips, refried beans, and great biscuits.

LEAF LARD

Leaf lard, also called flare fat, surrounds a pig's kidneys and is of very high quality. When rendered, it is one of the two main fats I use in pie dough, the other being butter. I consider the butter and leaf lard combination to make the best tasting and flakiest crust ever. Leaf lard enjoyed a revered place on the baking counter, until it was usurped in the early part of the 20th century by the brilliant "white as lard," "needs no refrigeration" marketing campaign of vegetable shortening. Shortening, now made with cottonseed and soybean oils, needs many processing steps to become a product with a somewhat indefinite lifespan requiring no refrigeration. If a fat needs no refrigeration I get the "skilly-wiggles," as Duncan's papa used to say. Manufactured lard that is found boxed on the grocery store shelf has also been processed with additives for shelf stability. Freshly rendered leaf lard is what you want. Please, don't let the words lard or fat put you off. Our brains need fat to function and leaf lard is a very good fat.

Look for rendered leaf lard at your local artisan butcher shop, or from the pork farmer at your farmers' market. If they don't have it, ask if they can get it for you, or have some shipped from an artisan renderer. (See Sources, page 338). If fresh un-rendered lard is what's available, it's quite easy to transform it into the precious substance that will help make your piecrusts flaky and flavorful in no time at all.

Select Bibliography and Books That Inspire

Amory, Cleveland, Lucius Beebe, the editors of American Heritage, et al. *The American Heritage Cookbook, Vol. 1* (Illustrated History) and Vol. 2 (Menus and Recipes). New York: Simon & Schuster, 1964.

Beach, Spencer Ambrose, Nathaniel Ogden Booth, and Orrin Morehouse Taylor. *Apples of New York*. 1–2 Vols. Albany: J. B. Lyon Company, 1905.

Beard, *James. James Beard's American Cookery*. Boston: Little Brown & Company, 1972.

Bell, Mrs. John. *Home Economics*. Astoria: Wickiup Grange, 1929.

Bender, Sue. *Everyday Sacred: A Woman's Journey Home*. San Francisco: Harper, 1995.

Beranbaum, Rose Levy. *The Pie and Pastry Bible*. New York: Scribner, 1998.

Berg, Elizabeth. T*he Day I Ate Whatever I Wanted*. New York: Ballantine Books, 2008.

Berolzheimer, Ruth. *250 Superb Pies and Pastries*. Chicago: Consolidated Book Publishers, 1950.

Bervin, Jen and Ron Silver. *Bubby's Homemade Pies*. New York: Houghton Mifflin Harcourt, 2007.

Brown, Dale, and the Editors of Time-Life Books. *American Cooking*. New York: Time-Life Books, 1971.

Brown, Edward Espe. *The Tassajara Bread Book*. Boulder: Shambhala, 1971.

Browning, Frank. *Apples: The Story of the Fruit of Temptation*. London: Penguin, 1999.

Bullock, Mrs. Helen. *The Williamsburg Art of Cookery*. Williamsburg (Colonial Williamsburg), distributed by Holt, Rinehart and Winston, 1966.

Child, Julia and Simone Beck. *Mastering the Art of French Cooking, Vol 2*. New York: Knopf, 1970.

Choate, Judith. *The Great American Pie Book*. New York: Simon & Schuster, 1992

Clarkson, Janet. *Pie: A Global History*. London: Reaktion Books, 2009.

Clayton, Jr., Bernard. T*he Complete Book of Pastry, Sweet and Savory*. New York: Simon & Schuster, 1981.

Colwin, Laurie. *Home Cooking*. New York: Knopf, 1988.

Cook's Illustrated, the editors of. *How to Make a Pie*. Boston: Boston Common Press, 1996.

Corriher, Shirley O. *BakeWise*. New York: Scribner 2008.

Cunningham, Marion. *Cooking with Children*. New York: Knopf, 1995.

———. *The Breakfast Book*. New York: Knopf, 1987.

Falaise, Maxime de la. *Seven Centuries of English Cooking*. New York: Grove Press, 1992.

Dimock, Anne. *Humble Pie*. Kansas City: Andrews McMeel Publishing, 2005.

Edge, John T. *Apple Pie: an American Story*. New York: G. P. Putnam's Sons, 2004.

Erschen, Olivia. *Cakes and Pastries at the Academy*. San Francisco: California Culinary Academy, 1993.

Gerken, Jonathan. *Apples I Have Eaten*. San Francisco: Chronicle, 2010.

Gillette, F. L. and Hugo Ziemann. *White House Cookbook*. Chicago: Werner Company, 1898.

Goldstein, Darra, ed. *The Oxford Companion to Sugar and Sweets*. New York: Oxford University Press, 2015.

Greenspan, Dorie. *Baking with Julia*. New York: William Morrow, 1996.

———. *Baking: From My Home to Yours*. New York: Houghton Mifflin Harcourt, 2006.

Haedrich, Ken. *Country Baking*. New York: Bantam, 1990.

———. *Dinner Pies*. Boston: Harvard Common Press, 2015.

Hamel, P. J., ed. *The King Arthur Flour Baker's Companion*. New York: The Countryman Press, 2003.

Harris, Florence La Ganke. *Pies A-Plenty*. New York: J. J. Barrows & Company, 1940.

Hibler, Janie. *The Berry Bible*. New York: William Morrow, 2004.

Hyam, Gina. *Pie Contest in a Box: Everything You Need to Know to Host a Pie Contest*. Kansas City: Andrews McMeel Publishing, 2011.

Jacobsen, Rowan. *Apples of Uncommon Character*. New York: Bloomsbury, 2014.

Kennedy, Teresa. *American Pie*. New York: Workman Publishing, 1984.

Kingsolver, Barbara. *Animal, Vegetable, Miracle*. New York: HarperCollins, 2007.

Konstanski, Pippi. *Pie Is Love: A Collection of Art Pies*. Bookemon (Self Published), 2011.

Le Draoulec, Pascale. *American Pie: Slices of Life (and Pie) from America's Back Road*. New York: Harper Perennial, 2003.

Lebo, Kate. *Pie School*. Seattle: Sasquatch Books, 2014.

Leonard, Jonathan Norton, and the Editors of Time-Life Books. *American Cooking: New England*. New York: Time-Life Books, 1970.

Longbotham, Lori. *Luscious Berry Desserts*. San Francisco: Chronicle Books, 2006.

MacPherson, John. *The Mystery Chef's Own Cookbook*. Philadelphia: The Blakiston Company, 1945.

McBirney, Nettie. *Aunt Chick's Pie*. Tulsa: The Chicadees, 1943.

McGee, Harold. *On Food and Cooking: The Science and Lore of the Kitchen*. New York: Scribner, 2004.

Nichols, Nell B. *Farm Journal's Complete Pie Cookbook*. Garden City: Doubleday & Company, 1965.

O'Neill, Molly, ed. *American Food Writing: An Anthology with Classic Recipes*. New York: Library of America, 2007.

Orsini, Elizabeth. *The Book of Pies*. London: Pan Macmillan, 1981.

Patent, Greg. *Baking in America: Traditional and Contemporary Favorites from the Past 200 Years*. Boston: Houghton Mifflin, 2002.

———. *A Baker's Odyssey: Celebrating Time-Honored Recipes from America's Rich Immigrant Heritage*. Hoboken: John Wiley & Sons, 2007.

Purdy, Susan. *As Easy As Pie*. New York: Atheneum, 1984.

———. *Pie in the Sky*. New York: William Morrow, 2005.

———. *The Perfect Pie*. New York: Broadway Books, 2000.

Rorer, Sarah Tyson Heston. *Mrs. Rorer's New Cook Book: A Manual of Housekeeping*. Philadelphia: Arnold and Company, 1902.

Ruhlman, Michael. *Ratio: The Simple Codes Behind the Craft of Everyday Cooking*. New York: Scribner, 2009.

Shaw, Patrick and Jenny Kostecki-Shaw. *Chai Pilgrimage*. Dancing Elephant Press, 2014.

Simmons, Amelia. *The First American Cookbook: A Facsimile of "American Cookery," 1796*. Mineola: Dover Publications, 1984.

Smith, Alisa and James MacKinnon. The 100-Mile Diet: A Year of Local Eating. Random House Canada, 2007.

Smith, Andrew F., ed. *The Oxford Companion to American Food and Drink*. New York: Oxford University Press, 2009.

Sokolov, Raymond. *Fading Feast: A Compendium of Disappearing American Regional Foods*. New York: Farrar Straus & Giroux, 1981.

Sokolov, Raymond. *The Cook's Canon: 101 Classic Recipes Everyone Should Know*. New York: William Morrow, 2003.

Steingarten, Jeffrey. *The Man Who Ate Everything*. New York: Knopf, 1997.

Strause, Monroe Boston. *Pie Marches On, 5th ed.* New York: Ahrens Book Company, 1963.

Swell, Barbara. *The Lost Art of Pie Making Made Easy*. Asheville: Native Ground Music, 2004.

Tannahill, Reay. *Food in History*. New York: Broadway Books, 1995.

Time-Life Books, the editors of. *Pies & Pastry*, Alexandria: Time-Life Books, 1981.

Traverso, Amy. *The Apple Lover's Cookbook*. New York: W. W. Norton & Company, 2011.

Weeks, Sarah. *Pie*. New York: Scholastic Press, 2011.

White, Patricia. *Pie!* New York: Simon & Schuster, 1969.

Willard, Pat. *Pie Every Day: Recipes and Slices of Life*. Chapel Hill: Algonquin Books, 1997.

Winslow, Marjorie. *Mud Pies and Other Recipes: A Cookbook for Dolls*. New York: Walker and Company, 1961.

Sources

All-Purpose Flour
· · ·˙·

BOB'S RED MILL
World Headquarters
13521 SE Pheasant Ct
Milwaukie, OR, 97222
800-349-2173
www.bobsredmill.com

KING ARTHUR
135 US Route 5 South
Norwich, Vermont 05055
800-827-6836
www.kingarthurflour.com

Gluten-Free Flours, Chia Seed, Flax Seed, Psyllium Powder
· · · ·

BOB'S RED MILL
World Headquarters
13521 SE Pheasant Ct
Milwaukie, OR, 97222
800-349-2173
www.bobsredmill.com

Butter, Cheeses, Irish Cream Liqueur
· · · ·

KERRYGOLD
Available US and Canada
kerrygoldusa.com/find_us

Vegan Substitute for Butter
· · · ·

EARTH BALANCE VEGAN BUTTERY STICK
Boulder, CO, 80302
201-421-3970
earthbalancenatural.com/store-finder/

Fresh Rendered Leaf Lard
· · · ·

DIETRICH'S MEATS AND COUNTRY STORE
660 Old Route 22
Krumsville, PA 19534
610-756-6344
www.dietrichsmeats.com

FANNIE & FLO
www.etsy.com/shop/FannieAndFlo

THE LARDIST
www.etsy.com/shop/Lardist

PRATHER RANCH
San Francisco Ferry Plaza and Farmers Markets
415-391-0420
prmeatco.com

BICHELMEYER MEATS
704 Cheyenne Avenue
Kansas City, Kansas 66105
913-342-5945

WAGSHAL'S
4845 Massachusetts Ave NW
Washington DC 20016
202-363-5698

Organic Peaches, Apricots, Nectarine, Plums, Pears, and Preserves
· · · ·

FROG HOLLOW FARM
Brentwood, CA 94513
888-779-4511 or 925-634-2845
www.froghollow.com

Spices
· · · ·

MARKET SPICE (IN THE PIKE MARKET)
85 A Pike Place
Seattle, WA 98101
206-622-6340
www.marketspice.com/store/category/bulk-spices

PENZEY'S
12001 W. Capitol Drive
Wauwatosa, WI 53222
800-741-7787
414-760-7337
www.penzeys.com
Stores and online

Apple Cider Vinegar
· · · ·

BRAGG'S APPLE CIDER VINEGAR
bragg.com
Grocery stores and online

Espresso Powder
· · · ·

MEDAGLIA D'ORO INSTANT ESPRESSO COFFEE
Grocery stores and online

Digital Scale
· · · ·

OXO
800-545-4411
www.oxo.com

Rolling Pins
· · · ·

FLETCHERS MILL
PO Box 268
1687 New Vineyard Rd
New Vineyard ME 04956
855-535-3824
http://www.fletchersmill.com

Pie Pans, Plates and Dishes
· · · ·

CERAMIC

EMILE HENRY
www.emilehenryusa.com

LE CREUSET
www.lecreuset.com

STAUB PIE PANS
www.staubusa.com

GLASS

PYREX
www.pyrexware.com/
800-999-3436

Pie Server
· · · ·

OXO
800-545-4411
www.oxo.com
Serrated on both sides, for righties and lefties

Pie Carrier
· · · ·

KWIK SEW ROUND CASSEROLE CARRIE PATTERN K3772
http://kwiksew.mccall.com/k3772-products
-20305.php
Downloadable Print Pattern Available

Culinary Equipment & Tools
· · · ·

SUR LA TABLE
84 Pine Street
Seattle, WA 98101
800-243-0852
www.surlatable.com

WILLIAMS SONOMA
3250 Van Ness Ave.
San Francisco, CA 94109
877.812.6235
www.williams-sonoma.com

Fruit Trees
· · · ·

RAINTREE NURSERY
Morton, WA 98356
800-391-8892
www.raintreenursery.com

ACKNOWLEDGMENTS

I am deeply indebted to many who have helped me along the pie way and in the creation of this book. To my editor, Ann Treistman, who sought out this country girl and believes in the power of pie. To book designer, Nick Caruso, a true genius and fine collaborator. To the incredibly kind and generous David Leite, who introduced me to my wonderful agent. To Joy Tutela, I believe in handshakes, too. To Andrew Scrivani, for your trust, belief, generosity, and talent; and to Soo-Jeong Kang for your vision on the shoot and in production. I am honored to work with you and call you friends.

To Kim Ricketts, who first knew that I had this book in me. If there is express mail delivery in heaven, you will receive the very first copy. I miss you every day. To Judy Amster, who has read each and every word I have written for years and continues to encourage me to write. To Toni Allegra, for your wisdom and generosity. To Rowan Jacobsen, Tara Austen Weaver, and Kim O'Donnel, each of whom told me that no one else could write this book but me. To Dorie Greenspan, for friendship and encouragement along the way. To chef and author Greg Atkinson, and writer and award winning pie maker Alicia Arter, thank you for your support and cheerleading in my early days of pie making and teaching.

To Ken Haedrich for advice and baking inspiration since the mid 80s when I was living in a tiny cabin and baking for my family from your books. To Jeanette Henderson and Andrew Behm for opening your kitchen so I could make pie with Ruth Reichl. To Merrilyn Sweeney for shamrocks and always having my back. I know that I am only here because of you. To Judith Dern whose generosity has no bounds. Thank you for always giving me a place to lay my head.

To Cathy Lynn Grossman who brought *USA Today* to the very first Pie Camp® and left as a close friend. To Annie Cobb and Michael Jayco for bringing Gretapie to my life. To Catherine Gewertz who opened her Bethesda home to me so I could first teach on the East Coast. To many others who have opened their homes and kitchens to me including

Kate Hill, Elise Bauer, Laura and Stewart Wilson, Anita and Cameron Crotty, Debi Koenig, Maren Christensen, Linda Nicholson, Betsy Taylor, Andy Smull, Yam Tolan, Rosalie Baker and the Clovis crew, Teri Turner, and Al and Becky Courschesne.

To Tess Masters who said, "If anyone can make a gluten free vegan dough, Kate, it's you." Your confidence in me got me through the six months it took to create it. To Jane Bonacci, Ilva Beretta, Jamie Schler, and Robin Ove, the best roommates in the world. To my webmaster Mary Walker who makes the Art of the Pie® website so beautiful. To my Facebook Pie Nation sisters and brothers. Thank you for being the best pie making community in the world. To Amy Chen for doing endless dishes and having the tenacity to keep making pie. To Traca Savadogo for a magical day on a rhubarb farm.

To Lance and Annetta Callin-Young who have encouraged me always to be true to myself. To Mary Alice Boulter for tequila and pecan pie. To Zorba Stricker for folding, steaks and good counsel. To Angel Lucas, a garden angel and true friend. To the Knitwits who tasted many pie experiments. To Jim Mader for turning my vision of Pie Cottage into a reality.

To the generations of pie makers who have come before me, especially Sadie Flynn, Vesta Marie Good Jackson, and Jackie Meek Potter, my first baking teachers who showed me that there are no mistakes in baking, just creative outcomes.

To Nancy Rivers, thank you for standing by me and carrying me when I no longer could.

To Maggie Finefrock, who has known me the longest and has unwaveringly believed in me. Thank you for the gift of pie-bys and being my north star.

And to Robin Jacobs and Duncan Graham, may your lives together be richly blessed with happiness and love.

CREDITS
· · · ·

Kate McDermott, Author/Food Stylist
Andrew Scrivani, Photographer

NEW YORK SHOOT
Soo-Jeong Kang, Prop Stylist
Miles Cohoe, Photo Assistant
Devon Knight, Photo Assistant

PIE COTTAGE, PORT ANGELES, WA SHOOT
Leigh Olson, Prop Stylist

Photo credit: Leigh Olson

INDEX